Liverpool
in the 1970s

Liverpool
in the 1970s

Phil Thompson

TEMPUS

This book is dedicated to the memory of the great Emlyn Hughes

First published 2005

Tempus Publishing Limited
The Mill, Brimscombe Port,
Stroud, Gloucestershire, GL5 2QG
www.tempus-publishing.com

British Library Cataloguing in Publication Data.
A catalogue record for this book is available from the British Library.

ISBN 0 7524 3431 4

Typesetting and origination by Tempus Publishing Limited.
Printed in Great Britain.

Contents

Introduction

The beginning of the 1970s saw the Pelé-inspired Brazil win the 1970 World Cup in scintillating style and in the process take football onto a higher plane. By the end of the decade Liverpool Football Club had firmly cemented their standing as one of the premier clubs in world football. After Everton's stunning 1970 title success it was expected to be they who would rule the roost on Merseyside for years to come, but the indomitable Bill Shankly had other ideas. With Anfield legends of the 1960s such as Roger Hunt, Ian St John and Ron Yeats making way for future Reds heroes such as Larry Lloyd, Steve Heighway and John Toshack, Shankly's second great Liverpool team was beginning to take shape.

Stalwarts of Shankly's great 1960s side such as Ian Callaghan, Tommy Smith and Chris Lawler would continue to give Liverpool great service throughout the early part of the 1970s and, in the case of Callaghan and Smith, would even star in Liverpool's first European Cup victory in 1977. It was three future England greats however, Emlyn Hughes, Ray Clemence and Kevin Keegan, who would prove to be the catalyst for what would eventually emerge in later years as probably the greatest Liverpool team of all time.

Former Manchester United and England star Steve Coppell would watch his heroes Liverpool from the Kop during this period and to him Hughes was the key element in Shankly's second great Liverpool side. Coppell said: 'Emlyn Hughes was at the heart of that outstanding Liverpool team of the 1970s. He seemed to grow in stature whenever he pulled on the Liverpool shirt.' Hughes' enthusiasm and will to win was infectious, and when Shankly introduced Kevin Keegan, a virtually unknown Yorkshire kid, into the Liverpool attack, a player whose enthusiasm would prove a match for even that of Hughes, the Anfield faithful knew they once again had a team to be reckoned with.

Right from the start of his Liverpool career Keegan was like a bundle of dynamite likely to explode in the opposition penalty area at any moment. Defenders found him a nightmare to defend against, with his incredible ability to slide past them with a dramatic burst of acceleration. The fearless Keegan kept up his breakneck pace for the whole of the ninety minutes' play. At the back, if any team did manage to break through Liverpool's almost impregnable defence they had the small matter of one of the greatest England goalkeepers of all time, Ray Clemence, to find a way past. Clemence was originally signed by Shankly from Scunthorpe in 1967 but the dependable Tommy Lawrence kept him out of the team until 1971 when Clemence became a permanent fixture in the Liverpool team. It had taken Bill Shankly a few seasons but the man who is credited with almost single-handedly turning Liverpool into a major force in British football had laid the foundations for a team that his heir apparent at Anfield, Bob Paisley, would turn into a world force.

Chapter One

Shankly's Second Great Team

The early part of the 1970s for Liverpool was a case of so near and yet so far as they came within a whisker of taking major honours in the English game. Season 1970/71 found them finishing a disappointing fifth place in the First Division, some fourteen points behind champions Arsenal. But Shankly was reconstructing his team and a Wembley FA Cup final against Arsenal gave Liverpool the opportunity to stop the London team completing the double and win some much-needed silverware for themselves in the process. The final was far from a classic and after ninety minutes of play the two teams had failed to score. Within two minutes of extra time starting Liverpool's up-and-coming wing star Steve Heighway put them into the lead. Liverpool were renowned for their solid defence and Shankly was confident that his second FA Cup would be coming to Anfield. Arsenal's Eddie Kelly then managed to scramble a scrappy equaliser and the double dream was back on. When Charlie George hit a sensational winner for the Londoners eight minutes from time, there was no way back for a Liverpool side that now looked tired and drained of energy on a warm May afternoon. Sitting in the stands witnessing Liverpool's defeat was their new signing Kevin Keegan. It would not be long before Keegan would galvanise the Anfield club into winning major honours of their own.

The following season Shankly's men would again miss out by the slimmest of margins, this time in the race for the League title. It was Brian Clough's Derby County who took the domestic game's major prize from Leeds, Liverpool and Manchester City, all just a single point behind the new champions. It was obvious for all to see that it would be only a matter of time before the glory days would return to Anfield again.

Season 1972/73 would prove to be a momentous one for Bill Shankly and Liverpool Football Club. It had always been Shankly's dream to produce a Liverpool team that could compete and win against some of the best opposition that Europe could offer. By the end of the season his team had not just won the League Championship, but in Europe they took the UEFA

Kevin Keegan with the man who brought him to Anfield, Bill Shankly. Keegan became the biggest superstar to hit English football since George Best in the 1960s. Newspapers and magazines inundated Keegan with offers for his services. Keegan once remarked: 'Shanks took a shine to me because I was from mining stock. My dad was a miner like Bill Shankly once was. He saw something in me that reminded him of himself at the same age. No-one can surpass Shanks for me, and I would put Bob Paisley level with him.'

Cup as well. In the process they had become the first English club to win the League title and a European trophy in the same season. Right through the team Liverpool had many players who showed exceptional form but the new darling of the Kop, Kevin Keegan, was simply irresistible. Keegan's goal tally for the season was 22. British football was beginning to see the emergence of a footballer who would rival 1960s icon George Best in the superstar stakes. His attacking partnership with John Toshack spread fear and trepidation in opposition defences with what has gone down in Anfield folklore as an almost telepathic understanding of each other's play.

Liverpool wrapped up the League title with a glorious 2-0 victory over their nearest rivals, Leeds United, on Easter Monday, 25 April 1973. Another outstanding Shankly signing, Peter Cormack, put them ahead against Don Revie's Leeds team and a second from Keegan was to prove decisive. At the end of the campaign Liverpool led the table by three points from Arsenal with Leeds seven points back in third spot. Many soccer pundits described Shankly's title-winning team as even better than the outstanding one the Scot had assembled in the 1960s, which was praise indeed. With the title in the bag there was to be no resting on their laurels as Shankly's men faced Borussia Mönchengladbach in a two-legged final of the UEFA Cup.

Liverpool's route to the final of the UEFA Cup began against Eintracht Frankfurt. The German team was expected to provide a strong test for Shankly's team, but goals from Keegan and Hughes at Anfield and a goalless draw in Germany saw them safely through to the next round. AEK Athens fared little better than Frankfurt and the Reds eased through 6-1 on aggregate. Dynamo Berlin were Liverpool's next opponents and a 3-1 aggregate victory gave the Anfield team an easy passage to the next round. Liverpool's quarter-final opponents were Dynamo Dresden. Goals from Hall and Boersma at Anfield and Keegan in the away leg saw Liverpool through to play Tottenham Hotspur in the semi-finals. Spurs were the current UEFA Cup holders and Liverpool were given the sternest of tests before taking their place in the final. An Alec Lindsay goal gave Liverpool a 1-0 victory at Anfield in the first leg, which was hardly enough to make the second leg at White Hart Lane a foregone conclusion. Two goals from Martin Peters gave Spurs a 2-1 victory but Heighway's away goal counted double and Liverpool were through to the final by the skin of their teeth.

The final against Borussia Mönchengladbach was over two legs, the first taking place at Anfield. Borussia would prove tough opponents and could boast top German internationals in their team such as Netzer, Bonhof and Vogts. The initial game at Anfield was actually abandoned with the score standing at 0-0

Kevin Keegan and Allan Clarke of Leeds United clash during a 1972 encounter. Tommy Smith, recalling Liverpool's games against Leeds during the 1970s, said: 'Sometimes the football went by the board. It was always a battle when we played Leeds.'

Following pages: *Tommy Smith and Larry Lloyd hold the League Championship trophy after the game against Leicester City in 1973. Smith captained Liverpool during their successful League campaign, and also to victory in the UEFA Cup during the same season.*

because of a torrential rainstorm. Bill Shankly noticed in the brief section of play that did take place that the Germans looked suspect against high balls and brought in John Toshack for the following night's replayed game. Shankly's ploy worked a treat and Toshack, with his extra height and heading ability, spread fear in the Borussia Mönchengladbach defence. Two goals from Keegan and one from Larry Lloyd gave Liverpool a comfortable 3-0 victory. The return leg was a much different affair with the Germans outplaying the Reds and winning the tie 2-0. Liverpool took the cup, however, 3-2 on aggregate to give Bill Shankly his first European trophy. It had been a long time in coming and Shankly was overjoyed to at last have his hands on some European silverware.

Emlyn Hughes hugs Liverpool boss Bill Shankly after winning the League title in 1973. Liverpool had won the title a few days earlier by defeating nearest rivals Leeds 2-0 on Easter Monday. This was the third and final League Championship of Shankly's managerial career at Anfield.

Emlyn Hughes and Phil Thompson celebrate in the dressing room after Liverpool's League Championship success in 1973.

Tommy Smith is presented with a good luck cake by Captain Wilf Preston, the pilot of the plane that flew the Liverpool team to Athens before their game against AEK Athens in the UEFA Cup 1972. Liverpool won the game 3-1 with goals from Hughes (2) and Boersma. They won the tie 6-1 on aggregate.

Steve Heighway

STEVE HEIGHWAY

Games:	444 (23)
Goals:	76
Honours	
European Cup:	1976/77, 1977/78
UEFA Cup:	1972/73, 1975/76
League Championship:	1972/73, 1975/76, 1976/77, 1978/79
FA Cup:	1973/74
34 Republic of Ireland caps (1970–1981)	

Steve Heighway was a key figure in Liverpool's fabulous trophy-winning decade of the 1970s. Born in Dublin, Heighway's parents were English, and the family moved back to England when the future Reds' star was ten. He was recommended to Liverpool coach Bob Paisley by Paisley's sons, who had noticed the flying winger tearing opposition defences apart in the colours of local amateur team Skelmersdale United. Paisley liked what he saw and advised the then Liverpool boss, Bill Shankly, to sign him. Heighway had also had a spell at Manchester City but turned down their offer to turn professional with the club. Heighway was keen to finish his university degree in politics and economics before turning his full attention to professional football.

Steve Heighway made his Liverpool debut against Mansfield Town in a League Cup replay in September 1970. Just a day later he made his international debut against Poland for Eire. His rise to the top was instant and Liverpool could not believe their luck that such a talented winger had been acquired for nothing. Apart from being a fast and skilful winger, Heighway was also capable of chipping in with vital goals on a regular basis. The Kop really warmed to Steve Heighway in a big way when he almost single-handedly turned the November 1970 Merseyside derby on its head with an incredible display of wing play at its best. With Everton two goals up and seemingly coasting to a comfortable victory, Steve Heighway moved into action and put Liverpool back into the game with a finely taken goal. He then sped past a couple of

Everton defenders and centred for Toshack to equalise for the Reds. When Chris Lawler put Liverpool 3-2 up, Anfield went ballistic. Liverpool fans were used to watching great wingers such as Ian Callaghan and Peter Thompson in action and in Steve Heighway they now had another to delight them.

Bill Shankly had always been keen to accommodate fast, skilful wingers in his teams and he once told the press after another scintillating Heighway display: 'That boy Steve Heighway can win a game with just one flash of genius.' Heighway's first season at Anfield ended in FA Cup disappointment with Arsenal beating them in extra time at Wembley after he had opened the scoring with a fine drive past Bob Wilson in the Arsenal goal. Shankly's team was on the verge of becoming a major footballing force again and the following season Steve Heighway picked up his first Anfield silverware with League Championship and UEFA Cup winners' medals. When Heighway's playing days at Liverpool came to a close, he had helped the Reds to win nine major trophies, the most notable being their first European Cup success in 1977.

By the time Steve Heighway left Liverpool to join Minnesota Kicks in 1981, the flying winger had played 444 games for the Reds, scoring 76 goals. First Division full-backs were glad to see the back of him, delighted that they would no longer have to spend a Saturday afternoon pondering on how to keep tabs on such a talented performer.

KEVIN KEEGAN

Games:	321
Goals:	100
Honours	
European Cup:	1976/77
UEFA Cup:	1972/73, 1975/76
League Championship:	1972/73, 1975/76, 1976/77
FA Cup:	1973/74
63 England caps (1972–1982)	

Kevin Keegan was arguably Bill Shankly's greatest signing for the Reds. Liverpool paid Scunthorpe just £35,000 for the Armthorpe-born forward.

Keegan signed for Scunthorpe as a sixteen-year-old in 1967. A year later he was offered a professional contract and, in the 1968/69 season, became a permanent fixture in the Scunthorpe first team. He quickly built up a reputation as one of the most talented youngsters plying their trade in the lower divisions. Many top teams sent their scouts to take a look at the Scunthorpe youngster, but it was Liverpool who took the plunge and he signed for the Reds in the spring of 1971.

After impressing in pre-season friendlies, most notably against Liverpool's Merseyside neighbours from across the water, New Brighton, Bill Shankly had no hesitation in handing Keegan his debut at the start of the 1971/72 campaign. Keegan scored after just seven minutes against Nottingham Forest on the opening day of the season in a 3-1 victory for the Reds. It was not just his goal, but Keegan's overall performance for Liverpool on that warm August afternoon that served notice to the Anfield faithful and the football fraternity in general that Shankly had captured a young player of incredible ability. Keegan would run himself into the ground for the whole ninety minutes and would leave experienced First Division defenders gasping for breath as they struggled to keep up with him. Bill Shankly had told the Yorkshire youngster during his first few weeks at Anfield that he was a certainty to play for England, and Keegan set out from the outset to make the Liverpool manager's prediction come true.

Kevin Keegan

During his first season at Anfield Keegan's form improved with every game and his all-action approach made him an instant hit with the Liverpool fans. Keegan's dynamic displays, coupled with his seemingly fearless attitude to taking on the First Division tough guys and often making monkeys of them with his explosive bursts of speed and excellent ball control, soon had the football media describing him as the greatest talent since George Best hit the headlines in the 1960s. Keegan's first season at Anfield finished trophy-less, but at the end of the 1972/73 campaign he was a League Championship and UEFA Cup winner. Although Liverpool had an outstanding all-round team, Keegan's partnership with John Toshack brought terror to First Division and European defences throughout the successful UEFA Cup and League Championship-winning 1972/73 season. It was also during this momentous season for Kevin Keegan that he won his first senior international cap, playing for England in a World Cup qualifying victory over Wales in Cardiff in November 1972.

English football's new superstar gave some of his most outstanding displays for Liverpool during their successful FA Cup campaign of 1973/74 season. Kevin scored probably his finest goal for the Reds with a superb volley against Leicester in their FA Cup semi-final replay against the Midlands team. Liverpool, inspired by Keegan, won the game 3-1 to set up a final against Newcastle. Kevin Keegan was simply sensational in the final itself and his two-goal salvo, coupled with his all-round display, confirmed to the watching nation that he was undoubtedly the greatest talent in English football.

More success for Keegan and Liverpool followed in successive seasons, culminating with the Reds' 1977 European Cup victory to cement Liverpool and Keegan's place amongst the elite of European football. When Kevin Keegan announced that he had decided to sign for SV Hamburg at the start of the 1977/78 season, Liverpool fans were bitter. He had served notice during the triumphant European Cup-winning season that he had made up his mind to ply his trade abroad, but they still found it hard to come to terms with his departure. However, Keegan's sensational six-year adventure at Anfield was to last longer in the memory than his at times acrimonious last season playing in front of Liverpool fans who could not bear the thought of him departing for pastures new. Today, Kevin Keegan is remembered fondly by those who saw him in the red of Liverpool as one of the all-time greats of Anfield history.

PETER CORMACK

Games:	168 (9)
Goals:	26
Honours	
UEFA Cup:	1972/73
League Championship:	1972/73, 1975/76
FA Cup:	1973/74
9 Scotland caps (1966-1972)	

Edinburgh-born Peter Cormack was signed from Nottingham Forest for a £110,000 fee in July 1972. Cormack had played 74 games for Forest, mainly as an inside forward. Cormack first came to Bill Shankly's attention when the Liverpool boss watched his international debut against Brazil in 1966. Shankly liked what he saw but it was not until six years later that he decided to take him to Anfield. Peter Cormack made his Liverpool debut against Derby County at the Baseball Ground in September 1972. Liverpool lost the game 2-1, but the Liverpool boss was impressed with Cormack's debut. The following week Cormack scored his first goal for the Reds in their 4-2 victory over Wolves.

Right from the outset Peter Cormack looked an outstanding acquisition to the Liverpool team with his skilful style of play, and he quickly gelled with Kevin Keegan. Cormack endeared himself to the Anfield faithful when he scored the only goal of the game to give Liverpool a 1-0 victory over Everton a few weeks after making his debut. Following Liverpool's derby victory Cormack was also on the scoresheet for Liverpool in their emphatic 6-1 aggregate victory against AEK Athens over two legs in the UEFA Cup.

The form of Peter Cormack was crucial in Liverpool's successful 1972/73 campaign when they won the UEFA Cup and the Football League title. In the League, Cormack netted 8 goals in 30 appearances, which was a useful total for someone operating mainly wide on the right of midfield. The following season found Cormack playing in a more central midfield role wearing the

Peter Cormack puts in a strong tackle against Spurs during a 1973 encounter against the London club.

number five shirt for most of the campaign. Liverpool ended the season as FA Cup winners. Injuries hit Peter Cormack's Liverpool career during the early years of Bob Paisley's period as manager, but he did pick up another League Championship winners' medal in the 1975/76 season. Cormack made 17 appearances for the Reds during their successful title-winning campaign. With his place in the Liverpool line-up no longer assured, Peter Cormack accepted an offer to join Bristol City in November 1976.

BRIAN HALL

Games:	196 (24)
Goals:	21
Honours	
UEFA Cup:	1972/73
League Championship:	1972/73
FA Cup:	1973/74

Brian Hall signed for Liverpool in July 1968. Born in Glasgow, Hall had trials for Blackburn, Bolton and Preston North End before accepting Bill Shankly's offer to join the Reds. He had to wait three years to get a chance in the Liverpool first team but when it did come he soon became a crowd favourite.

The Anfield faithful appreciated Hall's all-action style and total commitment to the Liverpool cause. Playing on the right of midfield, he formed a formidable partnership with Ian Callaghan when Shankly moved Callaghan into a more central position. Apart from being a hard worker, Hall was fiercely competitive and, allied to his impressive dribbling skills, this made him a valuable addition to the new team that Bill Shankly was building at Anfield.

Brian Hall proved his usefulness to the Liverpool cause by playing in 21 games during the League Championship-winning season of 1972/73. Hall also picked up a UEFA Cup winners' medal during the same campaign.

The following season, Brian Hall narrowly missed out on a second successive League Championship medal when Don Revie's Leeds United won the title with the Reds in second place. But in the FA Cup it was a different matter with Shankly's boys defeating Newcastle to take the trophy. Brian Hall was by this time a regular member of the Liverpool team and played in the majority of the fixtures in Bob Paisley's first season in charge.

Liverpool won the League title in Pais
Brian Hall making 13 appearances. But wi.
him for a place on the wide right, Hall kr.
numbered. Brian Hall accepted an offer from .
West Country in 1976.

Brian Hall

Chapter Two

Shankly's Swansong

Season 1973/74 would prove to be Bill Shankly's final one at Liverpool Football Club. His team had been expected to mount a strong challenge for the league, but it would be their old foes Leeds United who took the honours by five points from Liverpool in second spot. Shankly's farewell present to his beloved Liverpool faithful was the finest FA Cup final display in their history when they thrashed Newcastle United 3-0. The Newcastle team was full of top-class performers with Macdonald, Moncur, Smith and future Anfield greats McDermott and Kennedy in their line-up. But Liverpool tore them apart right from the kick-off in one of the most one-sided FA Cup finals of all-time. Two goals from Kevin Keegan, who was now an England regular, and one from Steve Heighway won the day for Liverpool.

Recalling the final, John Toshack said: 'For me that game was the culmination of things. The ground was suitable for playing football. I remember in one move we strung together twelve passes and on the thirteenth Kevin Keegan put the ball into the net.' Keegan himself said after the game: 'I'll never play in a game with that much atmosphere for the rest of my life, not even a World Cup final.' Newcastle's Terry McDermott was in the beaten team on that occasion, but would go on to taste many moments of glory himself in the red shirt of Liverpool. McDermott recalled: 'Keegan, Smith and Hughes: I was playing against my idols! You don't like to get beat in a final, but if you're going to get beat you'd choose that Liverpool team. We weren't even at the races.'

After their fantastic FA Cup triumph there was to be another notable honour for one of the Liverpool team that season when the hugely popular Ian Callaghan was selected as Footballer of the Year. The modest Callaghan was accompanied to collect his award by Bill Shankly. Callaghan recalled: 'It was great being the first Liverpool player to get the accolade, but I was so nervous. I looked along the table and saw some of the greats who had preceded me as Footballer of the Year. I nearly froze. Shanks said to me "You get out of this game what you put in, so enjoy the moment."'

Accompanying Ian Callaghan to London was, for Bill Shankly, one of his final tasks as boss of a club that looked to be on the verge of great things. His decision to retire from club management was announced at a press conference at Anfield on 12 July 1974. Many found it hard to believe, but once Shankly had made up his mind that was it. The debt that Liverpool Football Club owes to Bill Shankly in building it into a footballing power will never be forgotten by anyone at Anfield. But a new manager was quickly appointed, the man who would lead them to far greater glory on the field of play than even the legendary Shankly had achieved. That man was Bob Paisley.

Following pages: The Liverpool squad, 1974. From left to right, back row: Lawler, Boersma, Lloyd, Clemence, Layne, Toshack, Ray Kennedy, Thompson. Front row: Hall, Lindsay, Callaghan, Smith, Shankly (Manager), Hughes, Heighway, Cormack, Keegan.

Liverpool captain Emlyn Hughes chats to Princess Anne before the start of the 1974 FA Cup final. Emlyn and the princess were destined to become reacquainted a few years later on the BBC television programme A Question of Sport.

Kevin Keegan proudly holds the FA Cup aloft after Liverpool's 3-0 victory over Newcastle in the 1974 final. Bob Paisley said of Keegan: 'Kevin grafted as if his life depended on it. He made himself into an outstanding player. He recognised his limitations, and concentrated on getting the most out of the talent he possessed.' Keegan's England teammate, Sir Trevor Brooking, said about the Anfield legend: 'There have been more talented players than Kevin, but few to match his all-round ability. Whether ferreting in midfield or making space in the penalty area, he was a class act and a joy to work with.'

IAN CALLAGHAN

Games:	843 (5)
Goals:	69

Honours

European Cup:	1976/77
UEFA Cup:	1972/73, 1975/76

League Championship: 1963/64, 1965/66, 1972/73, 1975/76, 1976/77

Second Division Championship: 1961/62

FA Cup: 1964/65, 1973/74

4 England caps (1966–1977)

After signing for the Reds in 1957, Ian Callaghan was a first-team player at Anfield during their Second Division days. By the time he joined Swansea in 1978 Callaghan had made 843 appearances for Liverpool, a total, it is safe to say, that will never be surpassed. When people talk about the Anfield greats the name of Ian Callaghan tends to sometimes be overlooked, but not by the Anfield regulars who saw him, either on the wing or in later years in midfield, during the 1960s and 1970s. Although he was known as one of the gentlemen of football, teammates such as Tommy Smith insist that Callaghan could be as hard as most of the game's tough guys when the occasion demanded it.

During the 1960s Callaghan, along with Peter Thompson, would tear apart First Division defences with their dazzling wing play. Great Liverpool strikers of the era such as Roger Hunt, Ian St John and, in later years, John Toshack owed many of their goals to Callaghan's pinpoint crosses. Callaghan also possessed the ability to strike the ball with stunning ferocity. Examples of this include his goals against Everton in 1963 and Inter Milan in 1965. England boss Alf Ramsey included Callaghan in his 1966 World Cup squad and he played in one of the games leading up to the final. The success of Ramsey's team, however, with no recognised wingers in their line-up, meant that the likes of Ian Callaghan and Peter Thompson were never likely to become regular England internationals during the 1960s.

Ian Callaghan

At Liverpool it was a different story. Bill Shankly still wanted wingers in his team and Callaghan was an integral member of the great Liverpool teams that won the FA Cup in 1965 and the League Championship in 1964 and 1966. Indeed, it was Callaghan's precision cross that set up the goal for Ian St John to score the winner for the Reds in the 1965 FA Cup final against Leeds.

By the early 1970s Ian Callaghan had been allocated a new role for Liverpool in the centre of midfield. Brian Hall had taken over Callaghan's position on the wide right and was such a success that Bill Shankly, eager to keep one of his most consistent performers in his team, moved Callaghan into midfield. Callaghan took to his new position so well that he was even awarded further England caps to the couple that he had won in the mid-1960s. With Liverpool dominating the domestic scene in the 1970s, Ian Callaghan won a bagful of honours, culminating with the Reds' historic first European Cup victory in 1977. Emlyn Hughes said that Callaghan was his Man of the Match in the European Cup final in Rome against Borussia Mönchengladbach. Callaghan was accorded the accolade of becoming Liverpool's first ever Footballer of the Year in 1974. Just twelve months later he became Ian Callaghan MBE. Though never one to grab the headlines, Callaghan was a crucial member of the great teams that Bill Shankly and later Bob Paisley assembled at Liverpool in the 1960s and 1970s.

JOHN TOSHACK

Games:	236 (9)
Goals:	95
Honours	
UEFA Cup:	1972/73, 1975/76
League Championship:	1972/73, 1975/76, 1976/77
FA Cup:	1973/74
40 Wales caps (1969-1980)	

John Benjamin Toshack signed for the Reds in November 1970. Liverpool paid Cardiff £110,000 for his services. Toshack quickly rewarded Bill Shankly for bringing him to Merseyside by scoring the winner against Everton in a pulsating game that saw Liverpool fight back from 2-0 down to win 3-2. He had only been at the club a matter of days, but the Kop had found a new hero in just his second appearance for the Reds.

It wasn't until the following season when Kevin Keegan began to blossom as a Liverpool player, however, that John Toshack really began to display his obvious ability on a regular basis. Bill Shankly in fact dropped Toshack towards the end of 1971, but the Welshman's form in the Liverpool reserve team won him back his first-team spot. He had found the net 6 times in just 3 second-team appearances. Although he was dogged by injury on a regular basis, when he was fit the Toshack-Keegan partnership for Liverpool became a potent force for the Reds during the 1972/73 trophy-winning campaign.

Toshack's best goalscoring season for Liverpool came during the 1975/76 campaign when he knocked in 23 goals for the Reds. This goal tally included three hat-tricks, and Liverpool finished the season as League Champions and UEFA Cup winners. Kevin Keegan also scored his fair share of goals for the Reds during this period and many of his chances were set up by Toshack. The Welshman's heading ability was always one of his greatest assets and his superbly placed flicks to Keegan set up many a goal. In the triumphant UEFA

Cup run of 1975/76 season, Toshack also scored the crucial winner against Spanish giants Barcelona in the away leg of the semi-final.

The success that John Toshack enjoyed at Anfield might, in fact, have come to a premature end in 1974 when Bob Paisley agreed to sell him to Leicester for £160,000. Toshack failed his medical examination and Liverpool were left with no option other than to keep him at Anfield. It was a decision, however, that was to turn out to be somewhat fortuitous for the Reds, as Toshack was a key figure in many of their 1970s triumphs.

By the time that Toshack finally left Liverpool to take over as player-manager at Swansea City in 1978 he had played 236 times for the Reds, scoring 95 goals. He had won three League Championships, two UEFA Cups and an FA Cup. John Toshack also appeared for Wales on 40 occasions during his career. Although he played in some of the rounds of Liverpool's European Cup-winning season of 1976/77, Toshack was injured for the final. This robbed him of the chance of ending his Anfield career with the greatest European club medal of all.

John Toshack

ALEC LINDSAY

Games:	244 (2)
Goals:	18
Honours	
UEFA Cup:	1972/73
League Championship:	1972/73
FA Cup:	1973/74
4 England caps (1974)	

Alec Lindsay was signed by Bill Shankly from Bury in March 1969. The fee was £68,000. Lindsay had played in midfield for Bury but it was at full-back that he blossomed at Liverpool. During his first season at Anfield, Lindsay actually played as a striker in the Liverpool reserve team. He scored 22 goals but it was not a position he was happy playing in. A transfer request was handed in and it looked like Lindsay's Liverpool career was destined to come to a premature end. Shankly decided to try Lindsay in the left-back position that had proved so hard to fill since Gerry Byrne's retirement. It was to prove a success and Lindsay made the full-back spot his own.

England recognition in 1974 confirmed what most of the nation's football followers already knew. Alex Lindsay was the best left-back in England during this period and he looked destined for a long international career. The fact that he only went on to collect 4 England caps confirms the general opinion that Lindsay never quite fulfilled the high expectations that Liverpool had of him. The highlights of his Anfield career were undoubtedly in the 1973/74 season. During this period Alex Lindsay was a key member of the Liverpool team that won the UEFA Cup, the League Championship and 1974 FA Cup.

With his tough tackling and expert passing skills he was as crucial as any in the development of Bill Shankly's second great team at Anfield. However, after the highs of England recognition and FA Cup success in 1974, Alec Lindsay's form dipped in the following season and the emergence of Phil Neal and then Joey Jones in the left-back spot at Liverpool brought his Reds career to a close. Lindsay signed for Stoke City in 1977 after appearing 244 times for Liverpool.

Alec Lindsay

LARRY LLOYD

Games:	217
Goals:	5
Honours	
UEFA Cup:	1972/73
League Championship:	1972/73
4 England caps (1971–1980)	

Bristol-born Larry Lloyd signed for Liverpool in April 1969 for a £50,000 fee. Bill Shankly plucked Lloyd from Bristol Rovers, hoping that the giant centre half would eventually replace Ron Yeats at the heart of the Liverpool defence. Yeats was nearing the end of his magnificent Anfield career and a successor had to be found. When Liverpool noticed how well Lloyd had kept Everton's Joe Royle under control in an FA Cup-tie at Goodison Park, they thought they had found their man. Bill Shankly checked Lloyd out again when Bristol Rovers played at Tranmere, and the commanding centre half looked outstanding in a 2–1 victory for Bristol over the Merseyside club.

Larry Lloyd made the centre half position his own during the 1970/71 season, and a long career in the red of Liverpool looked assured. The sheer physical presence of Lloyd, allied to his fine heading ability and constructive use of the ball, caused many Liverpool fans to think that Ronnie Yeats had been replaced in the Reds' defence by an almost exact replica. The England selectors were also impressed by the massive defender and Lloyd won the first of his England caps in 1971. Larry Lloyd was an ever-present in the Liverpool team that won the League Championship in 1973. Lloyd also picked up a UEFA Cup winners' medal in the same season, and scored a vital goal against Borussia Mönchengladbach in the first leg of the final. His goal helped Liverpool to a 3–0 win.

The 1973/74 season turned out to be Larry Lloyd's last at Anfield. During the latter part of the campaign, Lloyd lost his place in the team through injury. Bill Shankly decided to try young Scouser Phil Thompson at the heart of the

Larry Lloyd

Reds' defence alongside Emlyn Hughes and it soon became apparent that this was a partnership made in heaven. Larry Lloyd failed to regain his place for the 1974 FA Cup final against Newcastle and, after Thompson's outstanding display for the Reds, Lloyd knew his Anfield days were numbered. Coventry City offered Liverpool £225,000 for the defender and his time at Liverpool came to an end. Larry Lloyd had played 217 games for the Reds.

Chapter Three

Bob Paisley
Takes Over

The squad of players that Bill Shankly left behind at Anfield, plus new signing Ray Kennedy, were understandably stunned when told that they would begin the 1974/75 season with Bob Paisley installed as manager. They were obviously happy to see Shankly's right–hand man promoted to the position rather than an outsider being brought in. Paisley was a popular man with the players and backroom staff alike, but could he manage? Kevin Keegan admits that the appointment of Paisley caused him some concern: 'When Bob got the job his first words were "I didn't want the job anyway." We didn't know whether to laugh or cry. I felt Bob was going to be set up as the fall guy. We were all worried about him because we liked him so much. But we felt that nobody outside the club would be daft enough to take the job on because of Liverpool's success.'

Bob Paisley might have been reluctant to take the Liverpool job but, after an initial season in control finding his managerial feet, there was to be no stopping him. Season 1974/75 proved to be fruitless for Liverpool on the trophy front, but several key ingredients had been added to the team. Ray Kennedy had been signed from Arsenal to play as a striker, but it was when Paisley converted him into a midfield role that his value to Liverpool began to grow. Full-back Phil Neal was also beginning to blossom into an outstanding defender, along with local lad Phil Thompson at the heart of the defence.

At the start of the 1975/76 season it was clear to Bob Paisley that his managerial role at the club was to be permanent. He had spent his first season thinking of himself as perhaps a stopgap until someone more qualified was installed as manager. When it dawned on Paisley that the person most qualified to manage Liverpool Football Club was in fact himself, he adapted into the job as if he had been doing it all his life. Paisley accepted the fact that he would never have the same rapport with the fans that Shankly had had, but nobody ever would. Once his team began winning silverware on a regular basis the Anfield faithful's affection for their new manager began to grow. After a tentative start to the new season Liverpool fought their way to the top of the table by Christmas. QPR pushed them all the way, but the title was clinched after victory over Wolves at Molineux in the final game of the season. Bob Paisley had won his first trophy

The Liverpool dressing room is a scene of joyous celebrations after the 1975/76 team clinched the League title with a 3-1 victory over Wolves in the final game of the season. Goals from Keegan, Toshack and Ray Kennedy, all in the last fifteen minutes of the game, brought the League Championship to Anfield. Recalling Liverpool's thrilling last-gasp victory, John Toshack said: 'It could not have been more dramatic if it had come out of a Boy's Own annual. I felt very proud that night and it remains one of the greatest moments of my career.' Ray Kennedy, who had also won major honours at Arsenal, said that winning the title with Liverpool was very special: 'This one means much more to me than when I was at Arsenal. I was too young to take it all in and appreciate it,' he said.

Kevin Keegan and Billy Bremner are sent off in an explosive Charity Shield encounter at Wembley in 1974. This was also Brian Clough's first game in charge at Leeds. The scene was set for a classic between the two best teams in the country. The first Charity Shield game to take place at Wembley, however, is remembered as one of the most violent clashes ever witnessed at the London venue. Within the first few minutes, Liverpool's Tommy Smith and Leeds' Allan Clarke had set the tone for the day with a couple of fearsome tackles. Liverpool's young defender Phil Thompson had received a gash from his ankle to his knee after one particularly nasty Clarke challenge and Liverpool, in particular Smith, wasted no time in exacting retribution against the Leeds forward. The major flashpoint of a match that was always threatening to explode out of control came in the sixtieth minute. Kevin Keegan was clipping at Johnny Giles' heels for the ball and the diminutive Leeds midfielder turned and hit Keegan with a right-hander that floored the Liverpool forward. Referee Bob Matthewson was obviously in a charitable mood and only booked Giles for his misdemeanour. Within minutes, Kevin Keegan and Billy Bremner became embroiled in a fist fight and Matthewson was left with no option other than to make Keegan and Bremner the first British players to be sent off at Wembley in the ground's history. The only other player previously dismissed at Wembley was the infamous Rattin of Argentina during the 1966 World Cup game against England. This was, in fact, Keegan's second dismissal in the space of five days. He was sent off against Kaiserslautern in a pre-season friendly prior to the Leeds game.

Further punch-ups followed, notably Ray Clemence against Joe Jordan, with Jordan's Leeds teammate Gordon McQueen joining in for good measure, but Keegan and Bremner were the only players to receive their marching orders. The game ended in a 1-1 draw, but Liverpool took the Charity Shield on penalties.

The sensational goings on at Wembley became the subject of newspaper headlines for weeks to come and was even debated by politicians in the House of Commons. Both Keegan and Bremner were to receive lengthy bans from the game plus a hefty fine. One disgusted television viewer (the game was broadcast live on TV for the first time) even tried to have Keegan and Bremner charged with breach of the peace, but could not find a magistrate who would issue a summons.

and he was overjoyed. He told the *Liverpool Echo*: 'This is the greatest night of my footballing life. Our success is based on firm foundations, which run right through the club. We have turned down the chance to sign players of ability because they don't have the character we are looking for. We play football in the Liverpool style, the style which wins trophies. Billy Shankly set high standards with great players. I would like to think he tutored me well. I've helped things along and cannot over-praise the help I've received from the coaching staff as well as the players. It is teamwork through all departments that makes Liverpool the club they are.' Emlyn Hughes said: 'On behalf of all the lads I want to tell the boss that we won this title for him.'

John Toshack had been on the verge of signing for Leicester City earlier in the season, but the midlands team were not happy with the Liverpool striker's medical report. He went on to play a key role in their title success. Toshack said: 'This championship win is the best thing that has ever happened to me at Liverpool. When the deal to Leicester City fell through people were saying that I was not capable of playing many games because of injury problems, but I've played 48 games this season.'

In 21 away games during their title-winning season goalkeeper Ray Clemence displayed outstanding form, letting in just 10 goals. Clemence was delighted to have yet another League Championship medal to add to his growing collection, but his mind was also on the UEFA Cup final in which Liverpool were due to play Belgian team FC Bruges over two legs. Clemence remarked: 'If we had not taken the title tonight we might have thought we could finish the season with nothing. Now the pressure is off I think we can win the UEFA Cup as well. This can be a springboard for cup success. We want to clinch the UEFA Cup and then I'd like to win the European Cup next season. That is probably our greatest ambition.'

Liverpool went on to win the UEFA Cup after two hard-fought games against Bruges. The first leg at Anfield was a sensational game with FC Bruges setting off at a storming pace to set up a 2-0 lead after just twelve minutes. The score stayed that way until the second half when relentless Liverpool pressure paid off with three goals in five minutes. Ray Kennedy pulled one goal back with a long-range drive. Jimmy Case scored Liverpool's second and Kevin Keegan completed a sensational comeback when he converted a penalty. John Toshack was taken off by Bob Paisley at half-time and replaced by Jimmy Case. The tactical switch paid off handsomely for the Liverpool boss and even Toshack himself acknowledged that Paisley was becoming a master tactician. Interviewed after the game Toshack said: 'I was bitterly disappointed at the substitution, but Bob has to be applauded for what happened. The Belgians had not allowed us to get near their penalty area, so any aerial threat I possessed had been completely nullified. A change of approach was needed. The scoreline was a tribute to the tactical knowledge of Bob Paisley as much as anything else.'

The second leg was equally as tension-packed as FC Bruges took an early lead, only for Keegan to quickly equalise for Liverpool from a free-kick. FC Bruges laid siege to the Liverpool goal with waves of attacks, but the Reds held firm to take their second UEFA Cup in four years. Bob Paisley had won two major trophies in just his second season in charge. Paisley had stated that Liverpool's greatest ambition was to bring the most prestigious club trophy of them all, the European Cup, to Anfield for the first time. Within twelve months that particular trophy would indeed be resting in the Liverpool trophy cabinet.

Kevin Keegan is seen here after receiving the Footballer of the Year award in 1976. During his acceptance speech Keegan said: 'I'm not the best player in the country by a mile, but I'm working on it.'

Liverpool captain Emlyn Hughes holds the UEFA Cup aloft after his team defeated Bruges 4-3 on aggregate in the 1976 competition. Hughes' teammate Ian Callaghan once remarked: 'Emlyn's enthusiasm was infectious.'

RAY CLEMENCE

Games:	656
Goals:	0
Honours	
European Cup:	1976/77, 1977/78, 1980/81
UEFA Cup:	1972/73, 1975/76
League Championship:	1972/73, 1975/76, 1976/77, 1978/79, 1979/80.
FA Cup:	1973/74
League Cup:	1980/81
61 England caps (1972–1983)	

Ray Clemence is the greatest goalkeeper in Liverpool's history. Bill Shankly signed him for just £18,000 from Scunthorpe in June 1967. Clemence had to wait a few seasons before taking over from Tommy Lawrence in the Liverpool goal. His debut was in January 1970 away at Nottingham Forest. The Reds lost 1-0, but Clemence made more appearances during the latter part of the season. By the start of the 1970/71 campaign he had made the position his own. Clemence's consistency was a key element in Bill Shankly's development of his second great team at Anfield in the early 1970s. During a remarkable eleven-season run, Ray Clemence missed just two games through injury.

Like most great goalkeepers, Ray Clemence improved as his run in the first team began to lengthen. His game did not appear to have a weakness and one of his greatest attributes was his total concentration. Clemence played behind an outstanding defence at Liverpool who gave the opposition few chances but when danger did appear it was rare for him to be caught napping. It was obvious from the start of his Liverpool career that Ray Clemence was destined to become an international goalkeeper. The only drawback for Clemence was the fact that another outstanding young 'keeper by the name of Peter Shilton had also forced his way into the England frame. Clemence, along with his Anfield teammate Kevin Keegan, made his England debut in November 1972 against Wales. It is hard to believe that

Ray Clemence

these two future England greats both started their football careers at Third Division Scunthorpe.

For the next decade Clemence and Shilton vied for the England goalkeeper position and, by the time his international career drew to a close, Ray Clemence had won 61 caps. At Liverpool, Clemence's position in goal looked impregnable. During one incredible season (1978/79) Clemence conceded just 16 League goals in 42 games. Clemence's 28 clean sheets during the that term remains a club record to this day. When Ray Clemence accepted Spurs' offer to move to the London club in 1981 after 656 appearances for the club, Liverpudlians probably realised that they were unlikely to have a goalkeeper of such outstanding ability guarding the Reds' goal again. They have, to date, been proved correct.

Ray Kennedy

RAY KENNEDY

Games:	381 (3)
Goals:	72
Honours	
European Cup:	1976/77, 1977/78, 1980/81
UEFA Cup:	1975/76
League Championship:	1975/76, 1976/77, 1978/79, 1979/80, 1981/82
League Cup:	1980/81
17 England caps (1976–1980)	

Ray Kennedy was Bill Shankly's last signing for Liverpool before Bob Paisley took over as manager at the start of the 1974/75 season. Kennedy cost Liverpool £180,000 from Arsenal and he was originally signed for his goal scoring ability. Although Kennedy missed the start of the new season through injury, when he did make the Liverpool line-up he knocked in 10 goals in 24 games. Kennedy had ousted John Toshack from the Liverpool front line but Paisley, towards the end of the season, began to experiment. He tried Ray Kennedy in a role playing behind Toshack and Keegan and it looked a promising combination. By the following season Kennedy had become a regular in the side, playing on the left of midfield. It turned out to be an inspired Paisley switch and Ray Kennedy went on to become a crucial element in the great Reds team that would win two European Cups in the 1970s.

Kennedy's passing ability, skill on the ball and powerhouse shooting ability soon had the Kop drooling and he became a firm favourite with the Anfield regulars. He could change the course of a match with one stunning pass, and his late runs into the opposition's penalty area often resulted in a crucial goal for the Reds. Kennedy's stunning form for Liverpool soon won him England recognition and between 1976 and 1980 he won 17 international caps. It was in Liverpool's European successes of the 1970s that Ray Kennedy often stood out and he was always capable of popping up with vital goals. Among the most memorable were his goals against Borussia Mönchengladbach in the semi-final of the European Cup in 1978 and in the semi-final of the same competition three years later against Bayern Munich.

The highlights of Ray Kennedy's Liverpool career were undoubtedly being part of the teams that won two European Cups in the late 1970s and 1981. After being converted into a midfielder he had become one of the game's leading players, and the midfield that he formed at Liverpool with Jimmy Case, Graeme Souness and Terry McDermott was probably the finest in the Reds' history. Like many of his Liverpool teammates, he decided to join John Toshack at Swansea in the early 1980s.

Phil Neal

PHIL NEAL

Games:	633 (2)
Goals:	60
Honours	
European Cup:	1976/77, 1977/78, 1980/81, 1983/84
UEFA Cup:	1975/76
League Championship:	1975/76, 1976/77, 1978/79, 1979/80, 1981/82, 1982/83, 1983/84
League Cup:	1980/81, 1981/82, 1982/83, 1983/84
50 England caps (1976–1983)	

Born in Irchester, Phil Neal was snapped up by Bob Paisley from Northampton Town for a £66,000 fee in October 1974. Neal was in fact Paisley's first signing for Liverpool, and what a bargain he turned out to be. Replacing Alec Lindsay for the Merseyside derby, Neal's assured display against Everton on his debut augured well for the future. The game ended in a 0-0 draw but Neal's performance was excellent. Phil Neal's second game for the Reds in December 1974 began a run of 366 first-team appearances, most of them playing at right-back. Neal rarely suffered from injuries and was a remarkably consistent performer who possessed all the qualities needed to become an international-class full-back.

Apart from his defensive skills, excellent positional play and outstanding distributional play, Neal was also a spot-kick specialist and most of his 60 goals for the Reds were from penalties. The England selectors soon began to make their way to Anfield to check out the outstanding full-back plying his trade in the red shirt of Liverpool, and Phil Neal made his England debut against Wales in March 1976. By the time his international career had come to an end, Neal had won 50 caps.

Liverpool's success in the 1970s is often put down to their remarkable consistency and there were none at Anfield more consistent than Phil Neal. He never seemed to have a bad game. When one considers his remarkable ability to keep up his high level of fitness, making 633 appearances for Liverpool in a ten-year period, he was in many ways the model professional.

Phil Neal's prowess as a penalty taker provided many crucial goals for Liverpool, none more so than his 1977 European Cup final goal against Borussia Mönchengladbach. He also scored a goal for the Reds, this time from open play, against Roma in the 1984 European Cup final. Always an attacking full-back, Neal also set up many a chance for his Liverpool teammates with the accuracy of his pinpoint crosses into the opponents' danger area.

By the time Phil Neal left Liverpool to join Bolton in 1985 he had accumulated an extensive collection of winners' medals from his Anfield career. It is highly unlikely that any future Liverpool player will ever succeed in surpassing the seven League Championship, four European Cup, four League Cup and one UEFA Cup haul of winners' medals that found their way back to the Neal household. When one considers that Paisley's first signing for the Reds cost less than what some present-day Liverpool players receive as a weekly wage, Phil Neal must go down as one of the greatest Anfield bargain buys of all time.

Chapter Four

Champions of Europe at Last

Liverpool embarked on the 1976/77 season determined to build upon what they had achieved the previous campaign and win not just the League title again, but the FA and European Cups as well. At the end of one of the most memorable seasons in the club's history they came within a whisker of pulling off this incredible treble of trophies. Bill Shankly's trophy-winning teams of the 1960s had, until this point, been generally acclaimed as the finest in the club's history, but now their 1970s counterparts were about to change all that. Ray Clemence was one of a new breed of stars at Anfield who were determined to eclipse what the 1960s teams achieved. He said: 'We were still a young side and for years we'd had it thrown at us that we'd never be as good as the 1964/65 team. But now we had an extra belief that we could go on to achieve even better things.'

Liverpool began the season with just two defeats in the first sixteen games. At Anfield they went through the entire season undefeated but away from home they won just five League games. Manchester City, Ipswich and Aston Villa pushed them for the League title all the way. It was, however, a fine end-of-season run with just two defeats from the beginning of February until the end of the campaign that enabled them to hang onto the championship.

In the FA Cup, wins over Crystal Palace, Carlisle, Oldham and Middlesbrough set up a semi-final against Everton. The Maine Road encounter proved a tense affair with Evertonians claiming that they were denied victory when referee Clive Thomas disallowed what appeared to be a perfectly good Brian Hamilton goal with the score standing at 2-2. Even Liverpool's John Toshack admitted after the game that the Blues were robbed. In the replay Liverpool cruised to an easy 3-0 victory to set up a Wembley final against Manchester United. Tommy Docherty's up-and-coming young team were expected to put up a strong challenge, but Liverpool were firm favourites to win the domestic 'double' for the first time in their history. In a memorable game United seized the initiative and opened the scoring through Stuart Pearson. Two minutes later Jimmy Case struck a fabulous equaliser, controlling a cross on his thigh before smashing an unstoppable shot past Alex Stepney in the United goal. Three minutes later Manchester United went back into the lead when Lou

Macari's shot hit Jimmy Greenhoff and looped over Clemence's head into the net. Liverpool fought back and Ray Kennedy almost equalised when his shot hit the United bar. United held on for a memorable victory and a dejected Liverpool team had just a few days to pick themselves up before the most important game in the club's history.

Liverpool's path to their first ever European Cup final appearance began in Northern Ireland against Crusaders. Goals from Neal and Toshack in the home leg made the away game a formality and as expected Liverpool took the tie with a comfortable 7-0 aggregate score. Trabzonspor of Turkey were their next opponents and, after losing the away leg 1-0, goals from Heighway, Johnson and Keegan set up one of the greatest nights in Anfield's history in the next round. Liverpool's opponents were French champions St Etienne and in the first leg it was St Etienne who were victorious, winning 1-0. The talismanic Kevin Keegan, who had been injured for the game in France, returned to the team for the home game. Ray Clemence recently described the St Etienne game as the noisiest, most atmospheric match that he ever played at Anfield. The French champions brought massive support to Liverpool and Anfield displayed the 'ground full' signs hours before kick-off took place. It was Kevin Keegan who sent Anfield into a frenzy after just two minutes when he latched onto a Heighway corner kick twenty-five yards out and lobbed the ball over the St Etienne goalkeeper Curkovic into the net. The crowd went crazy and willed their team to take the initiative and score a second. Despite periods of frantic Liverpool pressure it was the French side who scored next, early in the second half when Bathenay surged forward from his own half and beat Clemence with a long-range shot to the delight of the massed St Etienne supporters. Liverpool now had to score twice to reach the next round because of the away goals rule. Liverpool went back into the lead when Ray Kennedy ran onto a Toshack pass to shoot past the St Etienne goalkeeper. As the minutes

Following pages: *The Liverpool team that beat Southampton 1-0 in the 1976 Charity Shield. From left to right, back row: Toshack, Neal, Clemence, Heighway. Front row: Keegan, Callaghan, Hughes, Ray Kennedy, Case, Jones, Thompson.*

ticked by Liverpool sent on local boy David Fairclough for Toshack. With just six minutes to play the lanky Fairclough carved his name into Anfield folklore with a sensational goal. Kennedy put the ball through to him close to the halfway line. Fairclough then sprinted at the St Etienne defence from forty yards out. His dynamic burst of speed took him past several defenders before he slotted the ball past the advancing Curkovic to put Liverpool through. Anfield erupted as Fairclough was engulfed by his relieved teammates. It was one of the most important goals in the history of the club and it would be the highlight of Fairclough's Liverpool career.

Liverpool reached the 1977 European Cup final with a comfortable semi-final victory over FC Zurich. Phil Neal scored twice and Steve Heighway the other in Liverpool's 3-1 win in the first leg in Switzerland. The return leg was a formality with Jimmy Case scoring twice and Kevin Keegan the third in a 3-0 win. The Reds were through to their first European Cup final and their opponents were the talented German champions Borussia Mönchengladbach. The venue for the game was the Olympic Stadium in Rome.

After their shattering defeat to Manchester United in the FA Cup final, Bob Paisley was left with just a few days to lift his team for the most important game in Liverpool's history. Liverpool coach Ronnie Moran recalled the aftermath of the FA Cup final defeat. He said: 'We had to lift the players up right after the match. We'd won the League then lost to Manchester United in the FA Cup final. We decided to let the team have their night out. You have to let the players that want to let their steam out. We then went to the European Cup final in Rome. That was the big one.'

It was estimated that over 30,000 Liverpool fans made the trip to Rome to witness what would turn out to be a seminal night in the club's history. Paisley brought Ian Callaghan back into the team after dropping him in favour of David Johnson for the FA Cup final. Callaghan was, in fact, the only survivor of Liverpool's Second Division title-winning team of 1962. Along with Tommy Smith he was the only member of Shankly's great team of the 1960s who was still a first-team regular at Anfield. Callaghan, along with Smith, had an outstanding game against Borussia as Liverpool produced what was probably their best performance of the season. The Germans looked dangerous from the start and Bonhof was unlucky to see his shot beat Clemence but rebound from the upright in the early period of play. It was then Liverpool who took the initiative when Heighway set up McDermott, who curled the ball past the Borussia goalkeeper to put the Reds in front. Early in the second half Simonsen levelled the game when he scored from close range. Clemence was then forced to make an outstanding reflex save from Stielike to keep the scores level. Liverpool hit back and, from a Heighway corner, Smith, who was making his 600th appearance for the Reds, scored with a header to make the score 2-1. Kevin Keegan, who was playing his last game for Liverpool before joining SV Hamburg, had enjoyed an outstanding game against Germany's top full-back Berti Vogts and he forced the defender to concede a penalty when he upended Keegan in the box. Phil Neal stepped up to make the score 3-1 and send Liverpool's army of fans into ecstasy. Bob Paisley's dream of winning the European Cup had been achieved. Liverpool had for several seasons been the undoubted kings of the English game. They were now kings of European football.

Tommy Smith celebrates scoring Liverpool's second goal against Borussia Mönchengladbach in the 1977 European Cup final. Goals from McDermott, Smith and Neal gave Liverpool a 3-1 victory. Smith is joined in his celebration by Joey Jones and Jimmy Case.

Following pages: Kevin Keegan and Ray Clemence celebrate Liverpool's 1977 European Cup victory. 'It was the greatest night, ever!' remarked Clemence. John Toshack said that Keegan's display in the final was the greatest of his Anfield career: 'Kevin was tightly marked but he refused to be intimidated,' said Toshack. 'He simply got on with the game and gave his finest display in a Liverpool shirt.'

The glory of Rome 1977. Emlyn Hughes holds the European Cup aloft after Liverpool's 3-1 victory over German champions Borussia Mönchengladbach to win the trophy for the first time in their history. Hughes said after the game: 'When you walked out and saw the Italian Olympic Stadium packed with Reds fans, you could not even contemplate losing. Not when you saw how many had travelled over there from Liverpool. It was amazing, we just couldn't let them down.'

The Liverpool supporters celebrated long into the night both in Rome and back on Merseyside. The Liverpool side were quick to praise each other for their team's success. John Toshack, who was injured for the final, remarked: 'Kevin Keegan's display was his greatest in a Liverpool shirt. He refused to be intimidated and simply got on with the game.' Emlyn Hughes praised the veteran Ian Callaghan when he said: 'It was Cally who made the team tick. He was substitute for the FA Cup final but made all the difference when recovered for the European Cup final a few days later.' Ian Callaghan praised Keegan for his display and told the *Liverpool Echo*: 'It was a tremendous performance by the team and an unbelievable performance by Kevin Keegan in what was his last game for Liverpool. Kevin was special.' Former Liverpool legend Ian St John said: 'We wanted to win the European Cup for Shanks in the 1960s, but we didn't do it. To see two of our young guns Cally and Smithy in Rome winning the trophy was brilliant.'

Liverpool's magnificent victory was praised throughout Europe and the Italian newspaper the *Corriere Della Sera Milan* wrote: 'The victory of Liverpool was based on a constantly aggressive game, always on the attack, powerfully pressed by Kennedy, Callaghan and Case. They were always dangerous with a great showing by Kevin Keegan.' The British Prime Minister sent Liverpool a telegram that said: 'Please convey to all players and staff my warm congratulations on a magnificent achievement at the end of magnificent season. Best wishes Jim Callaghan.'

The magnitude of Liverpool's 1977 European Cup success was acclaimed recently at a celebratory reunion dinner for the heroes of the greatest night in the club's history. Bob Paisley's widow Jessie said: 'In 1977 you had to be champions of your country. Now you can finish second, third or fourth and still play in the Champions League. I don't care much for all these mini leagues. The knockout style was much more exciting. It wouldn't have been the same when David Fairclough came running through to score against St Etienne if he had known that his team had three or four other chances in the competition.'

Joey Jones, who was an underrated member of the 1977 side, told the *Liverpool Echo* of the joy he still feels when he reflects on that great night: 'What more could a fan ask for than to be a part of the team that won the club's first European Cup? Liverpool meant everything to me, it was the team I supported as a lad. I'm still a fanatical Red.'

JOEY JONES

Games:	97
Goals:	3
Honours	
European Cup:	1976/77
League Championship:	1975/76, 1976/77
72 Wales caps (1976–1986)	

Joey Jones was signed from Wrexham for £110,000 in July 1975. Bob Paisley hoped that Jones would take over at left-back in place of Alec Lindsay, who had suffered a loss of form, but the Liverpool boss felt that the Welsh defender was not quite ready for the Reds' first team on a regular basis. After a spell learning the Liverpool way in the reserve team, Jones made the left-back spot his own during the 1976/77 campaign. By now he looked like the finished article.

In his first season at Liverpool Joey Jones made enough first-team appearances to collect a First Division Championship medal and, in the following season, he won another League Championship, plus the big prize of a European Cup winners' medal as well. It was hard to believe that just two years before, Joey Jones was plying his trade in the lower divisions at Wrexham. Now he was a European Cup winner. As well as helping Liverpool to success in the League and in Europe with his fine displays in defence, Jones also began to pop up with vital goals, netting 3 times in League games. The highlight of Joey Jones' Liverpool career was undoubtedly being a part of the Reds' team that won the European Cup for the first time in 1977.

At a celebration dinner in 2002 held in Liverpool, Joey Jones was presented with the legendary banner that Reds fans displayed in Rome during their 1977 triumph. It read:

Joey ate the Frogs' legs
Made the Swiss roll
And munched Gladbach

Joey Jones in action against Manchester United in the 1977 FA Cup final. The United player is Jimmy Greenhoff.

The delighted Welshman told the press: 'Receiving this means as much to me as winning the medal. I couldn't believe when I read it at the game in Rome. When you think of all the stars in the Liverpool team, to play for the Reds was magic.'

Joey Jones' brief but spectacular Liverpool career came to an end in 1978 when he returned to Wrexham for a £20,000 fee.

David Fairclough

DAVID FAIRCLOUGH

Games:	88 (62)
Goals:	52
Honours	
European Cup:	1977/78
UEFA Cup:	1975/76
League Championship:	1975/76, 1976/77, 1979/80

David Fairclough signed for Liverpool in 1973 and made his first-team debut against Middlesbrough in November 1975. It was during the final weeks of the 1975/76 campaign that he began to make the Anfield regulars sit up and take notice with match-winning goals against Everton, Burnley and Stoke. He looked a certain star of the future with his uncanny knack of scoring vital goals. When called on for duty from the substitutes' bench, Fairclough looked a world beater and he quickly became known as 'Supersub.' Sadly his ability to make an impact over ninety minutes was never as great and his Reds' career became a somewhat disjointed affair.

After his match-winning performances in his first season for the Reds, great things were expected of David Fairclough at the start of the 1976/77 season. In domestic games, however, he failed to make the desired impact. He won a League Championship medal for the Reds but appeared in less than half the games. It was in the European Cup that the name of David Fairclough became enshrined into Anfield folklore during the 1976/77 campaign. Fairclough's stunning semi-final winner against St Etienne is still talked about to this day, but it was still not enough to win him a place in the Liverpool line-up for the final.

David Fairclough made up for his disappointment at not featuring in the 1977 European Cup-winning team by playing in the 1978 final of the competition. Fairclough and the Liverpool team enjoyed a 1–0 success over FC Bruges to take Europe's greatest prize for the second year in succession. Season 1978/79 ended with Liverpool winning another League Championship trophy, but Fairclough featured in just 4 games. The following year Liverpool won the title again. This time Fairclough played in 14 games scoring 5 goals. David Fairclough's failure to make a long-term impact at Anfield led to him trying his luck abroad and he signed for Canadian club Toronto Blizzard in 1982.

Tommy Smith

TOMMY SMITH

Games:	632 (1)
Goals:	48
Honours	
European Cup:	1976/77
UEFA Cup:	1972/73, 1975/76
League Championship:	1965/66, 1972/73, 1975/76, 1976/77
FA Cup:	1964/65, 1973/74
1 England cap (1971)	

Tommy Smith made the first of his 632 appearances for Liverpool against Birmingham in May 1963. Smith signed for the Reds as a fifteen-year-old and worked his way up through the ranks, Bill Shankly deciding to hand the young Liverpool-born player his First Division debut at home to the Midlands club. Tommy Smith soon became known for his fierce tackling and he was encouraged by the backroom staff at Anfield to fear no-one. Apart from his obvious ability and his will to win, what Shankly particularly liked about Smith was his versatility. He could play as an inside forward, a midfielder or in defence, and was equally good in all those positions.

Tommy Smith became an integral member of the first great team that Shankly assembled in the 1960s. Some have labelled him as just a destroyer who won most of his battles by frightening the opposition, but Smith's game had much more to it than that. There can be no doubt that Smith's tough streak came in useful in the hard days of the 1960s, when tackling from behind was still acceptable. But Smith also possessed the ability to read the game and this often came to his aid when facing opponents who had the beating of him when it came to pace.

It was always a source of great irritation to Bill Shankly that Tommy Smith never received the international recognition that his outstanding form in the early 1970s warranted. In 1971 Smith did receive his one and only England cap against Wales. He also came close to being voted Footballer of the Year, but was beaten to that accolade by Arsenal's Frank McLintock. Season 1972/73 was an outstanding one for Tommy Smith and he captained Liverpool to success in the League Championship and also the UEFA Cup. Smith's term of office captaining his beloved Liverpool came to an end the following season when Bill Shankly handed the captain's armband to Emlyn Hughes, a decision that did not go down at all well with the Reds' hard man. It looked like Tommy Smith's days at Anfield could be coming to an end, but an injury to Chris Lawler saw Smith back in the team playing at right-back.

Tommy Smith had enjoyed many outstanding moments during the Shankly and Paisley eras at Anfield, but the greatest of all came when he scored one of the Reds' goals in their 1977 European Cup triumph against Borussia Mönchengladbach. An injury to Phil Thompson led to Tommy Smith regaining his place in the team and he scored his famous headed goal against the German champions in his 600th appearance for Liverpool. The following season Tommy Smith again featured in Liverpool's successful European Cup campaign, but an accident while doing some DIY work at home caused him to miss the final against Bruges. Tommy Smith left Liverpool at the end of the 1977/78 season, after accepting John Toshack's offer to join him at Swansea.

After nearly two decades in the shirt of Liverpool, Anfield was never quite the same without the sight of Tommy Smith giving his all for the boys in red.

Chapter Five

King Kenny Sets Anfield on Fire

Liverpool began the 1977/78 season without the services of the man that Bill Shankly had brought to the club for peanuts but who was now the most-sought-after player in Europe. Kevin Keegan joined SV Hamburg in June 1977 for a fee of £500,000. Liverpool's search for Keegan's successor was solved when Bob Paisley wrote out a cheque for £440,000 to bring the player that many Liverpudlians claim is the greatest ever to wear the red shirt to Anfield. Kenny Dalglish was signed from Celtic at the start of the new season and typically scored within minutes of his League debut away to Middlesbrough. Dalglish and his family found Merseyside to their liking and were surprised at the friendly reception he received. He said: 'We felt safe in Liverpool. I remember getting off the train at Lime Street and walking the ten minutes to the Holiday Inn. The club put us up at the Holiday Inn while we looked for a house. I wouldn't have walked through Glasgow where the footballing rivalry has a nasty side.' Dalglish welcomed the down-to-earth atmosphere at Anfield with star treatment not being given to anyone at the club. Asked why he had chosen to leave Celtic where he enjoyed so much success, he replied: 'I left Celtic because I wanted to play for a team that was capable of winning in Europe.'

Liverpool had proved that they were easily capable of satisfying Dalglish's ambitions, with Bob Paisley's team striking fear into every other club on the Continent. There was even an early opportunity for the Reds to put one over on Kevin Keegan's new club SV Hamburg when they demolished them 6-0 in the second leg of the European Super Cup after holding them to a 1-1 draw in Germany. Goals from Thompson, Fairclough, Dalglish and a hat-trick from McDermott had the Kop chanting 'You should never have left Liverpool' at a bemused Kevin Keegan at the end of Liverpool's emphatic victory.

Apart from Dalglish, there were two other Scots signed by Paisley during this period when Alan Hansen in 1977 and Graeme Souness in early 1978 joined the Anfield ranks. Both would go on to become Liverpool greats. Hansen took a little time to become a first-team regular at Anfield, but Souness was an instant success. Domestically Liverpool just missed out on trophy success, finishing second in the League to Nottingham Forest and also being defeated by Brian Clough's team in the League Cup final after a replay. It was in Europe

Kevin Keegan signs for Hamburg in May 1977. He is watched by Liverpool chairman John Smith and SV Hamburg president Dr Peter Khrone. The fee was £500,000. With rumours of Keegan leaving Liverpool growing by the day, Bob Paisley told the Liverpool Echo: *'I don't want to lose Kevin but freedom of contract is looming and there could come a point if he wanted to go, he'd just go. He told me that if he went abroad he could be a millionaire in five years. You can't deprive him of that.' Kevin Keegan will always be remembered with great affection at Anfield.*

Legendary Liverpool manager Bob Paisley leads out his team alongside the Manchester United boss Dave Sexton. The occasion is the 1977 Charity Shield at Wembley which ended in a 0-0 draw. Bob Paisley is the most successful English manager of all time with thirteen major trophies, plus a European Super Cup to his name. Speaking about Paisley's incredible success, Kevin Keegan once said: 'Bob ended up winning so much, I don't think that anyone, not even Sir Alex Ferguson, will match it. It was a tremendous domination of the English and European game at a time when teams weren't doing that sort of thing. Bob was a fantastic guy. On a one-to-one basis he was full of stories and knowledge, not just about football, but things that you could relate to for the rest of your life.' When Paisley himself was asked about the secret of his success, he replied: 'Like Bill Shankly, I always felt that teamwork was most important. If you get too many individuals, some of them won't tie up with everybody else. They will still play as individuals and try to cut each other out. At Liverpool we always try to offload somebody like that. When you are buying players you must look closely at your team. It's that blend that you are after.'

Opposite: *Tommy Smith, together with tennis star Roger Taylor and Wales rugby union legend J.P.R. Williams, receive their MBEs at Buckingham Palace in 1977.*

Following pages: *Kenny Dalglish scores the winner against Bruges in the 1978 European Cup final. Dalglish once said: 'One of the reasons that I left Celtic in 1977 was because I wanted to play in a team that was capable of winning in Europe. Liverpool certainly satisfied that criteria. You wouldn't have imagined in your wildest dreams that they would be as successful as they were.'*

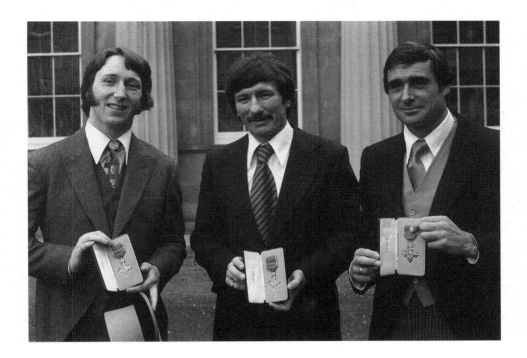

that they still reigned supreme, picking up a second European Cup. The early rounds of the competition saw them coast past Dynamo Dresden, Benfica and Borussia Mönchengladbach to reach their second consecutive final. Their opponents were Belgian champions FC Bruges. The final was played at Wembley, which gave them a significant advantage. FC Bruges appeared to be totally overawed by the Reds' home advantage and barely mounted an attack as Liverpool took the game to them. After a long period of probing the Bruges defence the Liverpool attack struck when Dalglish chipped the advancing FC Bruges goalkeeper Jensen to put his team into the lead. Liverpool did have one scare when Thompson cleared his lines, but in general they enjoyed total control. The Reds saw out the match without difficulty. It had been a poor final but few at Anfield cared. They had become the first British club to retain the European Cup.

Wembley was a mass of red and white as Liverpool captain Emlyn Hughes climbed the famous steps to lift the most sought-after trophy in European

football. Hughes told the *Daily Mirror* it was a moment he would never forget: 'There is no other sensation quite like it when you're handed a cup, turn, and then show it off to your adoring fans. I did it at Wembley when Liverpool won the European Cup in 1978. I remember looking and seeing the huge trophy glittering in the light from the floodlights. I wondered whether I would be able to lift it. But I was on such a high of excitement that I recall believing I could have lifted Red Rum above my head that night!' Liverpool goalscoring hero Kenny Dalglish remarked: 'My dream had always been European success. That goal was special to me because it meant me getting a winners' medal in a European Cup final. People who score the goals get the credit but in the same game Phil Thompson cleared one off the line. It could have been a wee bit problematic for us if we had finished 1-1. I was delighted with my medal and our season's work.' Alan Hansen was overjoyed to be a part of an historic occasion and could not believe that he was actually now in such a successful team: 'In previous years one European Cup final meant a six-pack in front of the telly with your mates, and there I was playing in one!' Terry McDermott had been a key element, with Graeme Souness and Ray Kennedy, of the Liverpool midfield that controlled the game. Though delighted to have won a second European Cup medal he was disappointed with the final: 'There was something missing in that game. FC Bruges went out looking for penalties. In a cup final you'd think both teams would go out to win. They just sat back and made it a nothing game.' Some in the game questioned the wisdom of bringing Kenny Dalglish down from Glasgow to replace Kevin Keegan, but he had proved to be an outstanding acquisition. Liverpool coach Ronnie Moran had no doubts that Dalglish would fit in at Anfield: 'Billy Shankly, Bob Paisley, Joe Fagan and Jock Stein, they were all in the same mould. They wanted players who were winners. We knew what kind of upbringing Kenny had had at Celtic under Jock Stein. He came to Liverpool and just slotted in. He must have been the bargain of the century. Kenny was a born winner. That's why he had so much success. He's a one off!'

Emlyn Hughes holds the European Cup after Liverpool's victory over FC Bruges at Wembley in 1978. Captaining Liverpool to European Cup success at Wembley was one of Hughes' proudest moments in a long, distinguished football career.

The triumphant Liverpool team parade the European Cup around Wembley in 1978. Kenny Dalglish recalled: 'What a party we had after the game! It started in daylight and finished in daylight.'

Opposite: Emlyn Hughes holds the European Cup high after Liverpool's defeat of FC Bruges in the 1978 final. Kevin Keegan said of Hughes: 'The word defeat did not exist in Emlyn's vocabulary. His will to win was what appealed most of all to our great managers Bill Shankly and Bob Paisley, and also to our supporters.'

Kenny Dalglish

KENNY DALGLISH

Games:	481 (16)
Goals:	168
Honours	
European Cup:	1977/78, 1980/81, 1983/84.
League Championship:	1978/79, 1979/80, 1981/82, 1982/83, 1983/84, 1985/86
FA Cup:	1985/86
League Cup:	1980/81, 1981/82, 1982/83, 1983/84
102 Scotland caps (1971–1987)	

Kenny Dalglish actually made his Liverpool debut against Southport 'A' team in August 1966. After the game, Bill Shankly and Reuben Bennett gave him a lift back to the YMCA in Liverpool where he was staying during his trial for the Reds. Shankly was keen to keep him at Anfield for a few more days to take a further look at him, but Dalglish had promised West Ham that he would give them the chance to run the rule over him and he set off for London. But the shy youngster was keen to return home to Glasgow and although Ron Greenwood, like Shankly, knew the fifteen-year old had something, it was for Glasgow Celtic that Dalglish signed professional forms in 1967. Liverpool fans can only dream about what might have been if Dalglish had joined the Reds in 1966 and the type of partnership he might have formed playing alongside Kevin Keegan at Anfield in the glory days of the 1970s.

Eventually, Liverpool did get their man when Kenny Dalglish signed for them in August 1977 for a British record fee of £440,000. It soon became apparent for all to see at Anfield that Liverpool had captured a fabulous player who was destined to take over Keegan's position as King of the Kop.

Legend has it that Bob Paisley told the Liverpool chairman, John Smith, that they had better get out of town as quick as possible after capturing Dalglish from Celtic. Paisley could not believe that the Glasgow club had actually allowed him to leave. Dalglish has been described as a footballing genius and the standard of play that he displayed for Liverpool during his career at the club saw him being acclaimed as the greatest player to ever wear the red shirt. Dalglish had everything; fantastic ball control, speed of thought, outstanding passing ability and the goalscoring touch of a Jimmy Greaves or Denis Law.

Kenny Dalglish had said that he had joined Liverpool because he hoped that he might win a European Cup with them. By the time he left he had won three European Cup winners' medals, plus a sackful of domestic honours. Dalglish showed right from the start of his Anfield career that he was a team player. It gave him as much pleasure to set up goalscoring opportunities for others as it did hitting the back of the net himself, which he did 168 times before his Liverpool days came to an end.

The highlight of Dalglish's early days at Liverpool in the late 1970s was scoring the winning goal against FC Bruges in the 1978 European Cup final at Wembley. In a tight match against the champions of Belgium, a fabulous piece of Dalglish opportunism, delicately chipping the FC Bruges goalkeeper for the only goal of the game, won the Scot a European Cup medal in his first season at the club. In 1979 Dalglish became the fourth Liverpool player to be elected as Footballer of the Year. The previous Reds who had won the award were Ian Callaghan, Kevin Keegan and Emlyn Hughes. Always the team player, Dalglish was keen to point out that his and Liverpool's success was built on the outstanding all-round team that Bob Paisley had assembled at Anfield. Liverpool's defence, for example, conceded just 16 goals in 42 games during the 1978/79 campaign. Summing up Kenny Dalglish's impact at the club, his teammate Phil Thompson once remarked: 'There was nobody to touch Kenny. He had the impossible job of replacing Kevin Keegan and became an even greater hero.'

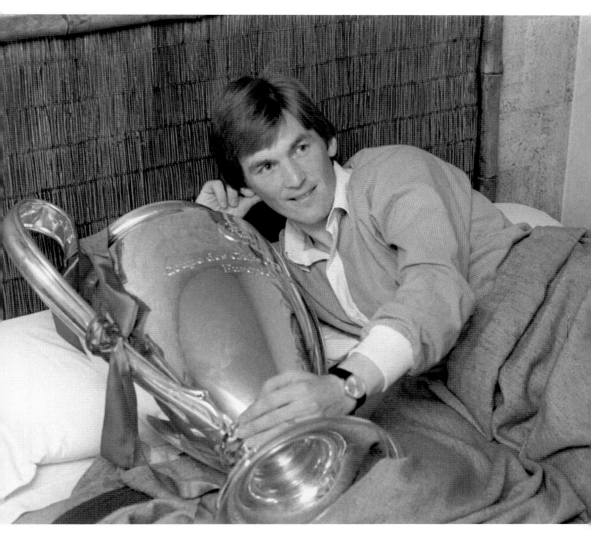

*Kenny Dalglish wakes up in his hotel room with the European Cup after Liverpool won the trophy in 1978.
Dalglish is considered by many to be Liverpool's greatest ever player. One of his Liverpool teammates in the
1970s, Steve Heighway, has no doubt at all that Dalglish was the best. Heighway said: 'Kenny was the best
player I ever played with. That's no disrespect to all the others at Liverpool. I've always told people that he
was the best because he had the complete range of skills. There are certain players you play with and you feel
that you will always win a game. You feel that your team will win because he is there in your team. If you
give that type of player responsibility you usually find that that type of player grabs it and says, 'Yes please,
I'll have that responsibility.'*

Emlyn Hughes

EMLYN HUGHES

Games:	657
Goals:	48
Honours	
European Cup:	1976/77, 1977/78
UEFA Cup:	1972/73, 1975/76
League Championship:	1972/73, 1975/76, 1976/77, 1978/79
FA Cup:	1973/74
62 England caps (1969-1980)	

The tragic death of Emlyn Hughes in November 2004 at the age of fifty-seven robbed Liverpool Football Club of one of its greatest sons. After a long battle with cancer, Emlyn died at his family home in Sheffield. Emlyn Hughes epitomised the great Liverpool teams of the 1970s with his boundless energy and enthusiasm. Like his great mentor Bill Shankly, Hughes was totally besotted with the game of football. For Hughes, like the great Shanks, there was only one way to play – to win.

Bill Shankly signed Emlyn Hughes from Blackpool in 1966. 'I knew Emlyn was a winner from the first time I saw him,' Shankly once said, and a winner Hughes undoubtedly turned out to be. Hughes' dynamic performances for Liverpool during his first season at the club soon had the Anfield faithful purring with pleasure. The Barrow-born youngster had everything. He was well built, could tackle like an ox, could fire in rasping shots at goal and had seemingly unlimited supplies of energy and stamina. There was also the added bonus that Hughes very rarely suffered from injuries. He had everything that Shankly was looking for in a player and at just £65,000 Liverpool secured from Blackpool one of the bargain buys of all time. Hughes made such an impact during his early days at Anfield that there were even rumours circulating that Liverpool's great rivals, Leeds United, had offered Shankly his pick of the Leeds team, plus cash, in a bid to secure Hughes' signature. Legend has it that Bill Shankly once informed a Lancashire policeman, who had stopped the Scot for having faulty lights on his car, that the future captain of England was sitting in the back seat. Shankly's prophecy was proved spot on when Hughes made his England debut against Holland in November 1969 and he later went on to captain his country.

Although Emlyn Hughes signed for Liverpool in 1967, his first silverware at the club did not arrive until five years later when the Reds won the League Championship and UEFA Cup in 1972/73 season. After that there was no stopping Liverpool and Emlyn Hughes, and if Charity Shield winners' medals are included he notched up an incredible fourteen-medal haul during his Anfield days. The highlight of Hughes' Liverpool career has to be captaining the Reds to their first European Cup success in 1977. By this time Hughes' marauding midfield days had become a thing of the past and for a number of seasons he formed an outstanding central defensive partnership alongside Phil Thompson.

When Emlyn Hughes held the European Cup aloft after Liverpool's 3-1 victory over Borussia Mönchengladbach in Rome in 1977, the broad smile on his face epitomised the joy at what Hughes and his teammates had achieved. Hughes was drunk with the sheer ecstasy of lifting the European Cup for his beloved Liverpool for the first time in the club's history. Hughes was to taste European Cup glory again in 1978 when Liverpool defeated FC Bruges at Wembley.

Emlyn Hughes left Liverpool in 1979 to join Wolves. He helped the Midlands team to win the League Cup in his first season at Molineux, the only trophy that he had failed to win during his Anfield days. Hughes finished his career playing at lower league clubs, but he will always be remembered first and foremost for his magnificent performances in the red shirt of Liverpool.

TERRY McDERMOTT

Games:	310 (12)
Goals:	75
Honours	
European Cup:	1976/77, 1977/78, 1980/81
League Championship:	1976/77, 1978/79, 1979/80, 1981/82
League Cup:	1980/81, 1981/82
25 England caps (1977–1982)	

Terry McDermott signed for Liverpool in November 1974. Bob Paisley liked the look of the Kirkby-born midfielder when Liverpool played Newcastle in the 1973/74 FA Cup final, and a £170,000 fee secured his services from the Magpies. It took McDermott some time to settle at Anfield, but when he did he became a tremendous midfield performer for the Reds. McDermott was similar in style to one of England's World Cup heroes, Martin Peters, in the way that he often arrived from deep positions into the opposition's penalty area unnoticed and scored some vital goals. It is often claimed that it was only when Graeme Souness joined the Reds that McDermott fully began to display his outstanding talent.

Terry McDermott was at his imperious best in the 7-0 annihilation of Spurs during the 1978/79 season. McDermott rounded off a fabulous Liverpool move that began in their own penalty area. The midfielder planted a firm header past the Spurs goalkeeper after sprinting the length of Anfield to get onto the end of Heighway's cross. McDermott made his England debut in 1978, in Ron Greenwood's first game as manager. He went on to make 25 international appearances. In season 1980/81 Terry McDermott was the top goalscorer at Anfield, hitting 13 goals including a hat-trick against Oulu Palloseura in the European Cup. McDermott also once hit a memorable hat-trick for the Reds in their 6-0 demolition of SV Hamburg in the 1977 European Super Cup.

In many ways Terry McDermott was the complete midfielder, with superb passing ability, tremendous stamina and fine goalscoring ability. Added to these

Terry McDermott

qualities was the toughness required to operate in the Liverpool midfield of the 1970s. With Graeme Souness, Jimmy Case and Ray Kennedy at his side, it was no wonder that McDermott and his Liverpool teammates were such an unstoppable force during this decade.

The highlights of Terry McDermott's Anfield career came during the 1979/80 season when, apart from winning the League Championship with Liverpool, he also collected two other prestigious awards. He became the first player to receive the PFA and Football Writers' Player of the Year awards in the same season. Bob Paisley was despatched to London to pick up the Footballer of the Year award on his behalf amid rumours that Terry McDermott had decided to spend the day attending a race meeting instead.

By the time McDermott signed for Newcastle in 1982 he had won a sackful of winners' medals in the red of Liverpool. In his 322 appearances he netted 75 goals.

Chapter Six

League Champions Again

Liverpool began the 1978/79 season hoping to record a hat-trick of European Cup wins. In the League they knew that reigning champions Nottingham Forest would be hard to depose. Brian Clough had built a tough and resilient outfit and he was also keen to emulate Paisley's success in European Competition, Ironically it was Forest who blunted Liverpool's hopes of a third European Cup when they defeated Paisley's men in the first round of the competition. In the first leg at the City Ground goals from Birtles and Barrett gave them a two-goal cushion to take Anfield for the return game. Liverpool threw everything at them in the home game but could not break down the Forest defence, and there was the outstanding Peter Shilton facing them in the Nottingham goal if they get did get a shot in. Forest held firm to force a 0-0 draw and Liverpool were out. The rise of Clough's team was complete when they went on to take Liverpool's crown, defeating Malmo in the final of the European Cup later in the season. In the League, however, Liverpool gained their revenge taking the title by an eight-point margin from Nottingham Forest with West Brom in third spot. Manager Bob Paisley was in his fortieth year with the club. He was voted Manager of the Year for a third season in a row and winning major trophies was now becoming second nature to him. Paisley told the press after his latest success: 'When I took over from Bill (Shankly) I said I hoped to win as many trophies as he did. I thought I'd be ninety-nine by then!'

The key to Liverpool's 1979 title success was the team's incredible defensive record at Anfield. In 21 home games they conceded just 4 goals. Away from home Ray Clemence was beaten just 12 times. In all League games he kept twenty-seven clean sheets. Clemence proudly told the press: 'I would like to think that it's one record that will never be beaten. We only conceded 4 goals at home all season. We felt we were unbeatable.' In attack Liverpool knocked in 85 with Dalglish and Johnson proving to be a prolific partnership with 37 goals between them. Graeme Souness played in many great teams at Anfield during his career but he reckons the 1978/79 side was the best of all. Souness said: 'I think the 1978/79 team was the strongest Liverpool team I have ever played in. They would take some beating. We approached games thinking how many goals we would win by today. That may sound cocky, but that's how it

Manchester United's Mickey Thomas lets fly with a free-kick against Liverpool in the 1979 FA Cup semi-final. United won the tie after a replay but went on to lose to Arsenal in the final.

was. When I joined Liverpool from Middlesbrough they were the team to join. They had just won the European Cup. They were a fantastic team in those days.'

Graeme Souness had proved himself to be an outstanding addition to the Liverpool team and Bob Paisley, in a 1985 interview for the *Sunday People*, told Brian Madley that Souness was in his opinion one of the greatest footballers to have represented the club. Paisley said: 'Graeme Souness was a real Jekyll and Hyde character. He's one of the most fearsome players I've ever seen but can also create poetry with his perfectly timed passes. He has a brilliant vision for space and an instinct for passing that few players possess. It was the way he disguised his intentions that gave Liverpool so much advantage.' With three exceptional Scots in their line-up in Souness, Hansen and Dalglish, Liverpool looked well to set to remain at the top for many years to come.

Opposite: *Liverpool manager Bob Paisley celebrates Liverpool's 3-0 victory over Aston Villa in May 1979. The Anfield boss had won his third League Championship in four years. Graeme Souness was a key figure in the Liverpool midfield during this period and when asked about the late 1970s line-up at Anfield, he said: 'The team was so strong and so confident. We could play football or we could mix it up when the pitches were not that great. In terms of football, that team would take some stopping. We could go anywhere in Europe and perform, when you think of the midfield of Kennedy, Case, McDermott and myself. The bigger the stage, the better the performance. You were surrounded by men. There weren't many battles we lost in those days.'*

Graeme Souness

GRAEME SOUNESS

Games:	350 (2)
Goals:	56
Honours	
European Cup:	1977/78, 1980/81, 1983/84
League Championship:	1978/79, 1979/80, 1981/82, 1982/83, 1983/84
League Cup:	1980/81, 1981/82, 1982/83, 1983/84
54 Scotland caps (1974–1986)	

Bob Paisley signed Graeme Souness from Middlesbrough for a £352,000 fee in January 1978. Souness became a true Liverpool great and, along with Kenny Dalglish, was a pivotal figure in the outstanding team that Paisley created in the late 1970s. Souness was the complete midfield player: ferocious in the tackle, a superb passer of the ball and with a thunderbolt of a shot. He scored many vital goals for the Reds throughout his career at Anfield and, by the time the 1970s had come to a close, had already picked up a European Cup medal and won two League Championships.

Graeme Souness made his Liverpool debut against West Bromwich Albion at The Hawthorns and David Johnson scored the winner for the Reds in a 1-0 victory. With Souness in their line-up alongside McDermott, Kennedy and Case, Liverpool now had a midfield that was the envy of football. Just a few weeks after his debut, Graeme Souness gave Anfield its first glimpse of his powerful shooting ability with a screamer against Manchester United to open the scoring for the Reds in a 3-1 victory. Ultimately, Liverpool missed out in the League Championship race, finishing seven points adrift of Nottingham Forest in second spot. Forest also beat the Reds in the final of the League Cup, but the sense of disappointment around Anfield was lifted when Liverpool won the European Cup for the second time in their history. In the final, Souness's through-ball to Kenny Dalglish set up the winning goal against FC Bruges.

The final two seasons of the 1970s saw Souness adding to his medal collection with Liverpool winning the League title in successive seasons.

During the 1978/79 campaign it was once again Nottingham Forest who pushed Liverpool all the way, along with Everton, but Paisley's team held on to give Souness his first championship medal. By the time Graeme Souness picked up his second championship honour in the 1979/80 season, he was being touted as one of the best midfielders in European football. Some pundits claimed that Souness lacked pace, but he more than made up for this with his superb all-round play and determination to win – sometimes at all costs. Joe Fagan once told a Liverpool scout that technique, first touch, vision, fitness, bravery, shooting and heading ability were not the only requirements needed to become a top Liverpool player: 'He has to be a f★★★ing winner', Fagan stressed over and over to the scout. Graeme Souness epitomised exactly what Joe Fagan was looking for when it came to meeting the requirements needed to become a Liverpool player during the golden days of the 1970s.

DAVID JOHNSON

Games:	174 (30)
Goals:	78
Honours	
European Cup:	1980/81
League Championship:	1976/77, 1978/79, 1979/80, 1981/82
8 England caps (1975–1980)	

David Johnson signed for Liverpool from Ipswich Town for a £200,000 fee in August 1976. Johnson began his professional career at Everton and signed for Ipswich in 1971. He established himself at Ipswich as one of the best strikers in the First Division. Paisley was keen to bring Johnson back to his native Merseyside to bolster Liverpool's defence of their League title and also to help in their bid to win the European Cup for the first time in their history. Johnson was an affirmed Liverpool fan and as a youngster would often cheer on his heroes from the Kop.

Delighted to be playing in the colours of his beloved Liverpool, David Johnson took a little time to become a permanent fixture in the Reds' team. A succession of injuries did not help his cause and in his first season at the club he had to settle for the substitutes' bench when Liverpool won their first European Cup at the end of the 1976/77 campaign. Johnson, however, did have the consolation of picking up a League Championship medal after playing 26 times for the Reds in their League games. The following season also did not work out as planned for Johnson, and a knee ligament injury caused him to miss out again when he had to sit and watch his teammates win their second consecutive European Cup at Wembley against FC Bruges. It was small consolation to Johnson that it was one of his goals that had helped Liverpool to victory in their 4-2 aggregative win over Borussia Mönchengladbach in the semi-final of the competition.

The 1978/79 season was to prove one of David Johnson's best at Anfield when he had a relatively injury-free run of games. His 16 goals in 30 League

David Johnson

games helped Liverpool to yet another title triumph. Johnson's partnership with Kenny Dalglish was now beginning to look outstanding, and between them they knocked in 37 goals as Liverpool romped to another League Championship success in the 1979/80 season.

Although David Johnson was eventually to lose his place in the Liverpool team to future Reds legend Ian Rush at the start of the 1980s, he did finally win a European Cup winners' medal in 1981. Johnson was a member of the team that defeated Real Madrid in the European Cup final held in Paris. His career at Liverpool may have been blighted by injuries, but Johnson still managed to net 78 goals in 174 starts for the Reds. His medal haul of four League Championship and one European Cup also makes impressive reading.

JIMMY CASE

Games:	236 (25)
Goals:	45
Honours	
European Cup:	1976/77, 1977/78, 1980/81
UEFA Cup:	1975/76
League Championship:	1975/76, 1976/77, 1978/79, 1979/80
League Cup:	1980/81

Jimmy Case was signed from non-League South Liverpool in 1973. The fee was just £500. He took a few seasons to force his way into the Reds' team, but by 1976 he had become a first-team regular. His debut was against Queens Park Rangers in April 1975 and he capped a fine display by forcing QPR's veteran defender David Webb into bringing him down to concede a penalty. With midfield players of the calibre of Graeme Souness, Terry McDermott and Ray Kennedy vying for places, securing a regular slot at Anfield was not easy, but Case figured in most of the Reds' key fixtures in their momentous 1976/77 season. In the semi-final second leg of their European Cup game against FC Zurich, Jimmy Case scored twice to give Liverpool a comfortable 6-1 victory over the two ties.

Jimmy Case played a key role in Liverpool's successful 1977 European Cup final against Borussia Mönchengladbach, helping to nullify the dangerous Borussia duo of Bonhof and Simonsen in midfield. Prior to the 1977 European Cup triumph Case had been Liverpool's Man of the Match in the FA Cup final defeat by Manchester United. When Case beat United goalkeeper Stepney with a superbly struck volley, most Reds fans thought their team would go on to win the trophy. But a mis-hit shot from Macari that hit Greenhoff and then ballooned over Clemence's head won the day for United.

Jimmy Case retained his place in the Liverpool line-up for the remainder of the 1970s and he won further honours in the 1977/78 season when the Reds retained the European Cup. Two more League Championships followed in

Jimmy Case

1978/79 and 1979/80. Case won a hat-trick of European Cup medals in 1981 when Liverpool defeated Real Madrid in the Paris final of the competition. He completed his medal haul at Anfield with a League Cup success over West Ham in the 1980/81 season. Jimmy Case took Graeme Souness's place in the Reds' team that beat West Ham 2-1 in the Villa Park replay.

Jimmy Case's Anfield days drew to a close when Sammy Lee forced his way into the Reds' team at the beginning of the 1980s. Case found that he had begun to spend a lot of time occupying the substitutes' bench. When Brighton offered Liverpool £350,000 to take him to the South Coast in 1981, Jimmy Case's Anfield days came to an end.

Chapter Seven

Paisley's Boys the Team of the Decade

Liverpool ended the 1970s with yet another title triumph. Once again Anfield proved to be a fortress as they went through the entire season unbeaten on their home patch. Emlyn Hughes, who had been a key player in so many trophy-winning seasons at Liverpool, had now joined Wolves. With Thompson and Hansen proving themselves to be a superb defensive partnership, Hughes' first-team appearances had become less frequent. Another Liverpool star that Bill Shankly had introduced into the first team, Steve Heighway, was also nearing the end of his Anfield playing career.

Liverpool began the 1979/80 campaign in unconvincing fashion with just two victories in their August and September fixtures. A run of sixteen games without defeat, however, took them to the top of the First Division. Liverpool stayed there until the end of the season and won the title by two points from Manchester United. In the cup competitions Liverpool were less convincing, with Dynamo Tbilisi knocking them out 4-2 on aggregate in the very first round. In the FA Cup Arsenal stopped them reaching Wembley after a marathon four matches in the semi-final. A goal from Brian Talbot in the third replay broke the Liverpudlians' hearts and set up an all-London final against the competition's eventual winners West Ham. In the League Cup Nottingham Forest would once again prove to be Liverpool's jinx team when they defeated the Reds at the semi-final stage. But Bob Paisley's fourth League title as manager certainly went a long way in making up for Liverpool's cup disappointments.

As the decade came to a close the world of football had come to recognise that the unassuming Paisley, the man who had told his squad of players that he didn't really want the job when Bill Shankly retired in 1974, had developed into one of the greatest managers that football had ever seen. Bob Paisley had always said that he would let his team do the talking for him. Paisley's teams in his period in charge at Liverpool certainly did his talking for him in some style as trophy followed trophy. When Emlyn Hughes told the press after Liverpool's title success in 1976 that the team 'had done it for Bob' you know he meant it. Paisley's football knowledge was considered by his players to be second to none. Kevin Keegan once said of Paisley: 'Bob treated us like men. What he had more than anything else was no ego. There wasn't anything wrong with Liverpool when Shanks left. It was a super run club in great shape. Bob just let the ship roll on. Bob said "Hey, I'm not changing anything, why should I? This place works. I know it well. I'm not changing anything. I know the players and I trust them. Let the ship sail on." And that is not easy to do. Everyone wants to put their mark on things. If you think of Brian Clough when he went to Leeds, he tried to change too many things. Bob didn't. He was a tremendous influence on everyone at that club.'

There is little doubt that the secret of Paisley's success at Liverpool in the 1970s was to keep the trophy-winning machine that Shankly had created at Anfield well oiled with little tinkering taking place. Paisley had no time for what he termed 'fancy dan' players. He preferred his players to keep it simple and work hard. The essence of Bob Paisley was that he was simple man with a superb football brain who believed that the game should be kept simple. Many in the game tried to emulate the Liverpool playing style but few succeeded. The 1970s had been a glorious decade for the Reds and with Bob Paisley at the helm everyone at Anfield was confident that their position at the forefront of the English game would remain unsurpassed for many years to come.

Phil Thompson

PHIL THOMPSON

Games:	459 (7)
Goals:	12
Honours	
European Cup:	1977/78, 1980/81
UEFA Cup:	1975/76
League Championship:	1972/73, 1975/76, 1976/77, 1978/79, 1979/80, 1981/82, 1982/83
FA Cup:	1973/74
League Cup:	1980/81, 1981/82
42 England caps (1976–1982)	

Liverpool-born Phil Thompson supported the Reds from the Kop as a youngster. Bill Shankly handed him his debut in April 1972 against Manchester United at Old Trafford. Thompson came on as a substitute for John Toshack in Liverpool's 3-0 victory over United. It was to be his only first-team appearance that season but the following year saw him pick up the first of many winners' medals for the Reds when he played enough games to qualify for a League Championship medal. For the next decade Thompson became a permanent fixture, playing as a central defender alongside Emlyn Hughes, Tommy Smith and, in later years, Alan Hansen.

Phil Thompson really came into his own as a Liverpool player during the 1973/74 season where his partnership with Emlyn Hughes really began to blossom. Liverpool failed to retain their League title but in the FA Cup they were awesome. In the final itself, Thompson had an outstanding game, completely cutting out the goalscoring threat of Newcastle's Malcolm Macdonald and John Tudor. After the game, Phil Thompson found it hard to believe that he was now an integral part of his beloved Liverpool team that, just a few years before, he had worshipped from the Anfield terraces. Though never a towering, hard defender in the Yeats or Larry Lloyd mould, Thompson made up for his lack of beef with his fine positional play. His reading of the game made him an exceptionally hard defender to get the better of, and he brought many an opposition attack to an abrupt end with a superbly timed interception.

International recognition was inevitable and Phil Thompson made his England debut against Wales in March 1976. Thompson, along with his Liverpool teammates Phil Neal, Ray Clemence, Kevin Keegan and Ray Kennedy, was delighted to be part of the England team that won 2-1. Thompson completed a memorable season by obtaining his second League Championship medal at the end of the 1975/76 campaign. This turned out to be his second winners' medal of the season after Liverpool defeated FC Bruges over two legs to win the UEFA Cup. It is interesting to note that during Liverpool's UEFA Cup campaign Thompson scored 2 of only 12 goals that he was to score during his Liverpool career. One of these goals was a crucial one against Barcelona in the semi-final second leg at Anfield to put Liverpool into the final.

Phil Thompson was jinxed by injuries during the 1976/77 season and, although he picked up another League Championship medal, he missed out on Liverpool's European Cup success. He could only sit and watch as Emlyn Hughes held the trophy aloft after the Reds' stunning victory in the final. Although he was delighted to see his team win Europe's greatest prize, he desperately wanted to be a part of such an historic occasion. The following season, however, Thompson was a key member of the Liverpool side that retained the trophy with a 1-0 victory over FC Bruges. By the time Liverpool won the European Cup for a third time, Phil Thompson was now captaining the team and, after defeating Real Madrid 1-0 in the final held in Paris, the kid from Kirkby proudly held the trophy aloft. By this time Thompson's partner in the centre of the Reds' defence was Alan Hansen. Phil Thompson had become an England regular and had even captained his country on several occasions. His first stint as England captain, however, was a game to forget as Thompson scored an own goal in England's 4-1 defeat against Wales in Wrexham.

Phil Thompson went on to collect more medals at Liverpool before his Anfield days came to an end. Injuries meant that his place in the Reds' defence became less secure. When Liverpool signed the outstanding Mark Lawrenson from Brighton towards the end of 1981, it was inevitable that he would be vying with Thompson to play alongside Alan Hansen when everyone was injury-free. After giving Liverpool twelve years' magnificent service, Phil Thompson signed for Sheffield United during the 1984/85 season.

ALAN KENNEDY

Games:	347 (2)
Goals:	21
Honours	
European Cup:	1980/81, 1983/84
League Championship:	1978/79, 1979/80, 1981/82, 1982/83, 1983/84
League Cup:	1980/81, 1981/82, 1982/83, 1983/84
2 England caps (1984)	

Alan Kennedy joined Liverpool for a £330,000 from Newcastle in August 1978. Born in Sunderland, he first came to Liverpool's notice during Newcastle's FA Cup campaign in 1974. Bob Paisley liked Kennedy's brave, tough-tackling style of play and his attacking instincts were an added bonus. Kennedy also had a powerful shot in his armoury and he soon became a crowd favourite. His wholehearted approach to football endeared him to the Anfield faithful, who nicknamed him 'Barney Rubble' after the *Flintstones* character.

In just his first season at the club Alan Kennedy picked up a League Championship winners' medal, playing in 37 games and scoring 3 goals. Liverpool's defence during the 1978/79 campaign was outstanding and they conceded just 16 goals. At Anfield, Alan Kennedy and his colleagues in the Liverpool defence allowed the opposition just 4 goals all season. The following season saw Alan Kennedy pick up another League Championship medal when he again featured in 37 games for the Reds. Once again Liverpool let in very few goals at home and remained unbeaten at Anfield for the second season in a row.

Although always keen to get forward in attacking positions, Alan Kennedy's goals tally at Liverpool was not as prodigious as it was expected to be when he first joined the club. All of this was forgotten, however, when he struck in the final of the 1981 European Cup, held in Paris. Latching onto a Ray Kennedy throw-in, Alan Kennedy ran at the Real Madrid defence that had held solid for eighty-three minutes and hit a rising shot past the Madrid goalkeeper for a sensational winner. This was undoubtedly the highlight of Alan Kennedy's career for the Reds. He eventually went on to sign for his hometown club, Sunderland, for a £100,000 fee in 1985 after making 347 appearances for Liverpool.

Alan Kennedy

ALAN HANSEN

Games:	604 (4)
Goals:	13
Honours	
European Cup:	1977/78, 1980/81, 1983/84
League Championship:	1978/79, 1979/80, 1981/82, 1982/83, 1983/84, 1985/86, 1987/88, 1989/90
FA Cup:	1985/86, 1988/89
League Cup:	1980/81, 1982/83, 1983/84
26 Scotland caps (1979-1987)	

Liverpool signed Alan Hansen from Partick Thistle for a £100,000 fee in May 1977. Hansen was an all-round sportsman who had already represented Scotland at basketball, squash, golf and volleyball while a youngster in his home country. He took a couple of seasons to settle down at Anfield but eventually replaced Emlyn Hughes at the heart of the Liverpool defence. Alongside Phil Thompson he established himself as a player of undoubted ability during the 1978/79 season.

A fine reader of the game, Hansen would break-up attacks with his shrewd positional play. It was soon noticeable that he possessed supreme confidence when he was under pressure and he made the art of defending look easy. Such was the effectiveness of the defensive partnership that Hansen, Thompson and the rest of the Liverpool defence formed in his first full season in the team that they only conceded 16 goals during the 1978/79 League campaign.

Alan Hansen's first honours in the Reds' team came in the European Cup triumph of 1978. Hansen had not expected to play in the final but did not let Liverpool down as they defeated FC Bruges 1-0 to take the trophy for the second year in succession. Although Hansen scored relatively few goals during his 604 games Liverpool career, he did manage to net one against Dynamo Dresden in the first round of that year's European Cup.

Alan Hansen's third major honour during his early years at Liverpool came in the 1979/80 season when the Reds retained the League Championship. Hansen played in 38 League games that season, scoring 4 times. The Scotland selectors also rewarded Alan Hansen for his fine performances at the heart of the Liverpool defence. He was awarded the first of his 26 Scotland caps in 1979.

Alan Hansen's Liverpool career drew to a close in the late 1980s. He had won practically every honour in the European game many times over. Fittingly, legendary Liverpool boss Bob Paisley once described Alan Hansen as 'the most skilful centre half I've ever seen in British football.'

Alan Hansen

Other titles published by Tempus

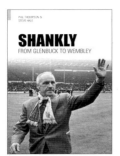

Shankly: From Glenbuck to Wembley

PHIL THOMPSON & STEVE HALE

Bill Shankly is the man who shaped Liverpool Football Club. His legendary status on Merseyside and within the history of the game cannot be overstated. Having been in charge at Carlisle, Grimsby, Workington and Huddersfield, he arrived at a struggling Liverpool in 1959 and transformed the club. This delightful illustrated biography records his life – from his birth in Glenbuck to the glory days when Shankly laid the foundations for Liverpool's rise to domination of the domestic and European football scene.

0 7524 2943 4

Wizards and Bravehearts: A History of the Scottish National Side

DAVID POTTER

The history of Scotland's national football team from 1872 is full of highs and lows, thrills and heartbreaks, passion and pride. Taking in thrilling World Cup campaigns and famous victories – notably over the Auld Enemy – the story has also featured many world-class players, such as Kenny Dalglish, Denis Law and Graeme Souness. This illustrated history records the ups and downs, the great characters and the classic games, and is essential reading for anyone with an interest in Scottish football.

0 7524 3183 8

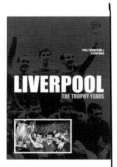

Liverpool: The Trophy Years

PHIL THOMPSON & STEVE HALE

Liverpool's haul of forty-five trophies to date makes them the most successful club in the history of English football. From the Second Division Championship of 1894 and through the halcyon days of the 1960s and '70s to the cup glory of the early twenty-first century, this book celebrates the triumphs and the players that achieved them. With text by Phil Thompson and photographs by the award-winning Steve Hale, it is an essential purchase for any follower of the Reds.

0 7524 2951 5

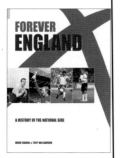

Forever England: A History of the National Side

MARK SHAOUL & TONY WILLIAMSON

This insightful and fascinating account, which covers the careers of England's all-time great players and the team's successes, failures and near misses, is an essential read for anyone interested in the history of the three lions. From the amateur gentlemen of the 1870s to the stars of the early twenty-first century, with many wonderfully evocative illustrations, it is the definitive history of England's national football team.

0 7524 2939 6

If you are interested in purchasing other books published by Tempus, or in case you have difficulty finding any Tempus books in your local bookshop, you can also place orders directly through our website

www.tempus-publishing.com